RUSHCLIFFE SCHOOL
BOUNDARY ROAD
WEST BRIDGFORD
NOTTINGHAM NG2 7BW

Revise for Geography GCSE OCR Syllabus C (Bristol Project)

0167

Liz Hattersley

NOTTINGHAMSHIRE EDUCATION COMMITTEE THE RUSHCLIFFE SCHOOL		
NAME	Form	Date of Issue
Sarah Underwood	11H	2nd march 2001
Selina Broan	11a	5/5/02
Ashley Barrington	11D	26/1/04
Karisma Patel	11U	13/05/05

Heinemann Educational Publishers
Halley Court
Jordan Hill
Oxford
OX2 8EJ

Heinemann is a registered trade mark of
Reed Educational & Professional Publishing Ltd

OXFORD   MELBOURNE   AUCKLAND
JOHANNESBURG   BLANTYRE   GABORONE
IBADAN   PORTSMOUTH NH (USA)   CHICAGO

Text © Liz Hattersley

First published 2000

02 01 00
10 9 8 7 6 5 4 3 2

All rights reserved. No part of this publication may be reproduced in any material form (including photocopying or storing it in any medium by electronic means and whether or not transiently or incidentally to some other use of this publication) without the prior written permission of the copyright owner, except in accordance with the provisions of the Copyright, Designs and Patents Act 1988 or under the terms of a licence issued by the Copyright Licensing Agency, 90 Tottenham Court Road, London W1P 9HE. Applications for the copyright owner's written permission to reproduce any part of this publication should be addressed to the publisher.

British Library Cataloguing in Publication Data
A catalogue record for this book is available from the British Library

ISBN 0 435 10105 6

Original illustrations © Heinemann Educational Publishers 2000

Designed, typeset and illustrated by Magnet Harlequin, Oxford

Printed and bound in the UK by Bath Colour Books

Acknowledgments
The publishers would like to thank the following for permission to reproduce copyright material.

Maps and extracts
p.23 David Waugh, The New Wider World / Thomas Nelson & Sons Limited, 1998; p.55 Mel Rockett, Themes in Human Geography / Thomas Nelson & Sons Limited, 1987; p.56 Corus (formerly British Steel); p.62 Paul Warburton, Tourism in Tanzania / Stanley Thornes (Publishers) Limited, 1990; p.103 © Third Way 1988 Reprinted by permission from the Christian current-affairs magazine Third Way; p.10 and 107 Maps reproduced from Ordnance Survey mapping with the permission of The Controller of Her Majesty's Stationery Office © Crown copyright, Licence no. 398020.

Photographs
p.43 NOAA; p.107 NRSC/Science Photo Library; p.109 Esa/pli/Science Photo Library; p.110 Still Pictures.

The publishers have made every effort to trace the copyright holders. However if any material has been overlooked or incorrectly acknowledged, we would be pleased to correct this at the earliest opportunity.

Tel: 01865 888058   www.heinemann.co.uk

Contents

	Page
Introduction	4
How to use this book	7
Theme 1: Physical systems and environments	9
Weathering	9
How does the sea shape the landscape?	10
How does ice shape the landscape?	12
The hydrological cycle	13
How do rivers shape the landscape?	16
Weather and climate	17
Climate change	22
Ecosystems: the Amazon rainforest	24
Theme 2: Natural hazards and people	29
Tectonic hazards: earthquakes and volcanoes	30
Floods	38
Drought	40
Tropical storms	42
Theme 3: Economic systems and development	46
Primary industry: farming	47
Secondary industry	53
Growth and decline of economic activity in an MEDC outside the EU	57
Regional growth and decline in the EU	59
The effects of economic change on the quality of life	62
Trade and investment	65
Unequal levels of development	66
Theme 4: Population and settlement	72
Population distribution	72
Population structure	75
Population change	77
Migration	80
The location of settlements	85
The settlement hierarchy	86
Declining settlements	87
Growth of rural settlements	88
Comparing regions	91
Places	93
DME and practical skills	96
The Decision Making Exercise	96
Practical skills	100
Reference section	107
Answers and advice on the exam	112
Exam technique: top tips	112
Matching case studies to questions	113
Answers to exam-practice questions	114
Index	120

Introduction

What is so special about Geography?

If you are reading this book you are probably approaching a GCSE exam in Geography. Geography helps us to understand our surroundings. The world is a beautiful place, coloured by a variety of cultures, beliefs and traditions. The world is diverse in terms of physical features, landscape and climate. It is this diversity which makes Geography so interesting. Our sense of place is created by a combination of social, physical and economic characteristics. While all places are unique, we can identify patterns and processes everywhere. By studying Geography you will become aware of these patterns and understand the processes that create them.

Perhaps more importantly you will learn that the world is a dynamic place – constantly changing in response to physical, social and economic processes. To understand, predict and prepare for these changes is very important. Geography gives you the opportunity to discover how lives can be affected by change. Only when we understand why these changes occur can we begin to control them. With informed decisions and careful consideration of the needs and values of the people involved we can help to shape our world and make it a better place for future generations.

OCR Syllabus C (Bristol Project)

This syllabus brings the study of Geography to life by exploring key themes and contemporary issues in the context of real places. You will study five themes which provide a broad framework for classroom based learning:
- Physical systems and environments
- Natural hazards and people
- Economic systems and development
- Population and settlement
- People's use of the Earth.

(Theme 5 in this book is not covered by a separate chapter, it is woven into the other chapters as in the textbook, *People, Places and Themes*.)

Each theme explores a number of related issues that combine to provide a thorough grounding in Geography. The syllabus aims to reintroduce the importance of place in Geography. Each theme is studied using real case studies about real issues and places, usually chosen by your teacher. The case studies must include local areas as well as the rest of the UK and the EU (European Union). They will also include an MEDC (More Economically Developed Country) from outside the EU and a named LEDC (Less Economically Developed Country).

Assessment: What will be expected from you?

You will be expected to show knowledge of the five themes outlined above with reference to specific places you have studied. It is very important that you have a clear idea of the case studies your school has chosen.

Your knowledge, understanding and skills will be assessed in three sections:
1 Coursework   25%
2 DME (Decision Making Exercise)   25%
3 Terminal examination   50%

1 Coursework

You will have to complete two pieces of coursework worth 10 per cent of the final mark, and a geographical investigation worth 15 per cent of the final mark. The coursework will be based on three sub-themes:
1 Processes that shape and change the landscape
2 Land use within settlements
3 An environmental or planning issue.

At least two of these sub-themes must be based on your local area so you can use your local knowledge to support your work.

Your coursework gives you an opportunity to show your understanding of the patterns and processes involved. You will also be expected to show competent use of fieldwork skills such as data collection, mapping, and field sketching. Analytical skills such as the interpretation of maps, photographs and satellite images will also be tested. An ability to present and communicate your findings clearly and accurately is essential.

2 The Decision Making Exercise

The DME will assess theme five – People's use of the Earth. It is a formal examination which takes place in the Spring term. The exercise asks you to explore an environmental issue in depth using a variety of resources. A resource pack is available before the examination so you can explore the issue in greater depth. Candidates are expected to use this time to study the resources so they can refer to them with confidence to support their answers.

The DME is an interesting and stimulating method of assessment. Further information on this element of the course and advice on preparation for it is included on page 103.

3 Terminal examination

The terminal exam offers a two tier entry system. The Foundation paper awards C–G grades; the Higher paper awards A*–D grades. Both papers have the same basic structure. Each paper has two sections.

Section A focuses on places and you should show your knowledge of the themes within the context of places. There are three questions in section A (numbered 1–3), based on the EU, MEDCs and LEDCs:
A1 This question is about the EU and UK.
A2 This question is about LEDCs.
A3 This question is about MEDCs outside the EU.

Section B contains four questions (numbered 4–7) on themes 1 to 4. You must show clear knowledge of the themes making references to real places in your answers:
B4 This question is about physical systems and environments.
B5 This question is about natural hazards and people.
B6 This question is about economic systems and development.
B7 This question is about population and settlement.

You must answer four questions in total. Two must be chosen from section A and two from section B – one from B4 or B5, and one from B6 and B7.

Each question is worth 20 marks, awarded for skills, knowledge and understanding. Questions will tend to follow a standard format. Of the 20 marks:
a) and b) are both worth 2 marks each and often test your interpretation of resources using skills. You should aim to spend approximately three minutes on each of a) and b).
c) and d) are both worth 4 marks each and often ask you to use skills and knowledge to describe and explain patterns relating to the resource. You should aim to spend about six minutes on each of c) and d).
e) is worth 8 marks and usually, but not always, tests knowledge and recall of specific case studies. You should aim to spend approximately 12 minutes on this section.

You have 30 minutes for each of the major questions. Try not to go over this time – it will give you too little time for the last question. You will be expected to use a variety of resources which may include a colour photograph, an OS map extract and/or a satellite image (see pages 114-120). These will be provided for you in the exam. Each question will have a range of question styles allowing for both short and more extended answers.

Understanding exam questions

Knowledge and understanding is essential to succeed in examinations. However, you must also know how to use this knowledge when answering specific questions. Every year students lose marks through not answering the actual question set. The OCR syllabus requires you to know, and be able to respond accurately to, the following command words:

Annotate	Add notes or explanations to labels on a map or diagram.
Comment	Give your educated views on something.
Compare	Give the similarities and differences between two or more examples.
Describe	Write about what something is like.
Draw	Illustrate your answer with an appropriate labelled diagram.
Explain	Write about why or how things occur.
Give reasons for…	Give more than one possible explanation for something.
Identify	Select or pick out relevant information.
Justify	Give your reasons for….
Label	Identify and name features of a map or diagram.
List	Give a number of short concise facts or observations.
Locate	Describe where something is in relation to other places.
Predict	Suggest what might occur in the future based on the evidence available.
Select	Choose from a number of options.

State	Give a short, clear response.
Study	Look carefully at something before answering a question.
Suggest	Write down what you think based on your current knowledge and understanding.
Summarise	Write down the main points.
Use	Refer to something in your answer.

For examples of how these command words may be used in examinations refer to page 122 (matching case studies to questions).

Preparing for exams

Good preparation for your exams is essential if you are to do yourself justice. People have found many different ways to revise and prepare for exams. Everybody has a method they feel comfortable with. Before you begin your revision it is important you know what you have to do and why you have to do it.

The term 'revision' means simply to look again at the work you have already done. For many people this is done merely by re-reading old notes. Some people will spend hours re-writing notes or underlining sections of work. For some lucky people this is sufficient but for many this method leaves them badly underprepared for their exams.

Just re-reading your notes has many drawbacks as a form of revision:

- If your notes are incomplete you may be failing to learn important work.
- If you did not fully understand the work at the time it is unlikely to become clearer just by re-reading or summarising.
- Re-reading may help you to remember your notes but it will not help you to fully understand the issues.
- You may still find it difficult to apply your knowledge and understanding to new and unfamiliar circumstances such as an exam question.

As you can see passive methods such as this can lead to poor exam performance, so what can you do about it? GET ACTIVE!

Good exam preparation demands an active approach. You must view this period like a bank account. You have to put something in before you can get anything out. Of course, if you put more in you can get more back! If you are prepared to work hard and invest some time and energy, exam success can be yours. This revision guide will help you develop an active approach to exam preparation. It is not just a book full of the information you need to know to pass the exam. It is a tool designed to help you revise the course within a clear structure, learn the information required, and develop the skills needed to successfully answer exam-style questions. Don't forget that you can also use your textbook when you are revising, and you can ask your teacher for help.

How to use this book

To get the most out of using this book you should also have the following things available:
- Your class work notes
- A notebook
- Your textbook and relevant handouts from your teacher.

This guide is divided into four main chapters on the four major themes in the syllabus. Each chapter studies a variety of places from within the EU, LEDCs and non-EU/MEDCs. The fifth theme has been integrated into all four chapters and is assessed through the Decision Making Exercise. There is a chapter on the Decision Making Exercise and practical skills. There is no specific order in which you need to study the chapters but you should revise all of them within your preparation period. You will probably find some easier than others. Try not to spend too much time on the parts you feel comfortable with. It is the sections that you find more challenging that you need to focus on.

Throughout the book there are hints and tips to improve your revision and examination technique. Special notes are included on the right hand side of most of the pages in the book. You have already come across some of these:

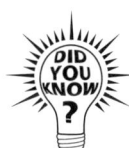 Extra information and useful facts and ideas to help you with your examination answers.

Hints and Tips! These give general advice and useful information to help you prepare for and sit the examination. Following the advice could stop you wasting time and improve your grade.

Themes

Places

Things to do: boxes to tick to check your progress, gaps to fill in, activities to focus your revision to improve that grade. If you do well, be pleased with yourself. If at first you don't do well, re-read the section and test yourself again. These cover the themes in the course and also ask you questions on the places you have studied.

All the chapters include some examination practice questions similar to those you will face in the final examination. Higher Paper and Foundation Paper questions have been provided. Each question includes the number of marks you can hope to achieve. At the back of the book you will find answers to the exam practice questions and lots of other useful advice on the best way to answer questions – and even how not to answer them!

Step by step revision

Step 1 Choose the theme you wish to study. Begin by studying your own notes. Sort out your work into clear sections and make a note in your notebook of any areas you find difficult or unclear.

Step 2 Read the relevant section of this guide. This may help to clarify some of those problem areas and fill any gaps in your notes.

Step 3 Test yourself using the 'Test Yourself' questions (without looking up the answers in the text). Reward yourself for successes but think carefully about mistakes. Do you know where you went wrong? Do you understand the correct answer? If there are areas you feel unsure of go back and study them again.

Step 4 The first test will demonstrate your short-term memory; try the tests again a week later. How much have you forgotten?

Step 5 When you feel confident that you have learnt the sections thoroughly try to apply your knowledge and understanding to the exam-style questions provided at the end of each chapter.

Keep a record of what you have covered using the tick list provided at the end of each chapter. Be honest with yourself; if you do not feel confident with a topic you must make an effort to improve.

You have many exams to prepare for and you must make time for all of them. With this in mind you should attempt to cover one main chapter of this book in a week. The whole book should therefore be covered in about five weeks. Of course you might need to adjust this time to match your personal workload. Try using the timetable on page 8 to structure your revision.

Revise for Geography GCSE

Table 1 – Revision timetable

	Week 1	Week 2	Week 3	Week 4	Week 5	Week 6
Monday						
Tuesday						
Wednesday						
Thursday						
Friday						
Saturday						
Sunday						

Theme 1: Physical systems and environments

Weathering, erosion, transport and deposition

For this theme you will need to know about:
- the **processes** associated with rivers, ice and the sea
- weather and climate
- physical environments and systems.

Key Ideas
- Landscapes are formed over time by the continual action of **geomorphic** processes.
- Physical processes of the Earth's crust, atmosphere, and biological activity are all acting to:
  i) break down the fabric of the land
  ii) transport weathered material
  iii) deposit debris elsewhere.

Key words and definitions
geomorphology	The shaping and changing of the landscape.
weathering	The breakdown of rocks where they are found.
mass movement	The down slope movement of the Earth's surface due to gravity.
erosion	The wearing away and transportation of the land by wind, water or ice.
scree	Rock fragments, loosened by weathering, on the sides of valleys

Weathering

There are several types of **weathering**. Geographers classify them in three groups:

1) *Physical weathering* The breakdown of rocks by mechanical forces.
- **Freeze-thaw action** occurs when water seeps into joints and cracks in rocks and freezes. The freezing water expands by approximately 10 per cent and exerts tremendous pressure on the surrounding rock. The rock will crack and fragments may fall off forming **scree**.
- **Exfoliation (onion skin weathering)** occurs when the surface of rocks is weakened by continual expanding and contracting as temperatures rise and fall during the day. The surface layer cracks and peels away leaving the layer below open to weathering. This is usually evident in desert regions.

2) *Chemical weathering* Rock decay by chemical reactions such as carbonation, hydrolysis, and oxidation.
- **Carbonation** occurs in rocks with a high content of calcium carbonate such as limestone and chalk. Carbon dioxide from the atmosphere combines with water to produce a weak acid called carbonic acid. This acid reacts with the calcium carbonate to form calcium bicarbonate. Calcium bicarbonate is soluble – the rock is dissolved and carried away. This form of weathering is common in the Yorkshire Dales and produces landforms such as caves, limestone pavements and sinkholes.

3) *Biological weathering* The breakdown of rocks by the action of plants and animals.
- **Root growth** can exert tremendous pressure on rocks causing them to weaken and crack.
- **Animals** can also cause weathering by burrowing.

How does the sea shape the landscape?

Key Idea
- We can study coastal landscapes in terms of erosion, transportation and deposition.

Key words and definitions
fetch — The distance wind travels across open water.
permeable rock — Rock which allows water to soak through.

Coastal erosion

The coast is under constant attack from the sea. As the wind travels across the sea it creates waves. As the waves enter shallow water the base is slowed down by increased friction, the crest of the wave topples forward and the wave 'breaks' onto the shore. The energy released by a breaking wave is enormous and can have a significant impact on coastal landscapes. The strength of a wave depends on two factors:
1. The length of the **fetch**, i.e. the distance wind travels across open water.
2. The speed and duration of the wind: faster winds blowing persistently will produce stronger waves.

There are four processes responsible for coastal erosion, all of which are accelerated by stronger seas.
1. **Hydraulic action** Air and water are forced into cracks and joints creating pressure that breaks up the rock.
2. **Corrasion** The waves carry eroded material backward and forwards grinding the rock away.
3. **Attrition** The eroded material is ground together, gradually smoothing off rough edges and reducing the size of particles.
4. **Corrosion** Salt water dissolves the mineral structure of rock.

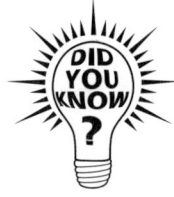

Did you know?
The type of rock affects the rate of coastal erosion. The mineral composition, the degree of jointing, the permeability will all affect the rock's resistance to erosion. Weak, highly jointed, **permeable rocks** will erode more quickly than harder, more resistant rocks. The weak rocks are eroded to form bays while the more resistant rocks form headlands.

▲ *Hydraulic action as waves crash against cliffs*

Hints and Tips!
Using the terms – hydraulic action, corrosion, corrasion and attrition in your answer – rather than just writing about erosion generally, will gain you more marks.

How does the sea shape the landscape?

Transportation of eroded material by the sea

Key Idea
- Waves have the power to transport millions of tonnes of sediment. The movement of sediment depends on the type of wave and the direction of approach.

Key words and definitions
swash	The movement of a wave up the beach.
backwash	The movement of a wave back down the beach.
longshore drift	The transportation of sediment along the beach in the direction of dominant waves.

As a wave breaks onto a beach it runs up the beach. This flow of water is called the **swash**. As the wave loses energy it flows back down the beach, this is called the **backwash**. The strength of the swash and backwash affects the movement of sediment on the beach. As waves lose energy, they deposit their load.

If waves approach the coast at an angle the swash carries sediment up and across the beach. The backwash will flow back at right angles to the coastline. As a result sediment is moved along the beach with each wave. This process is called **longshore drift**.

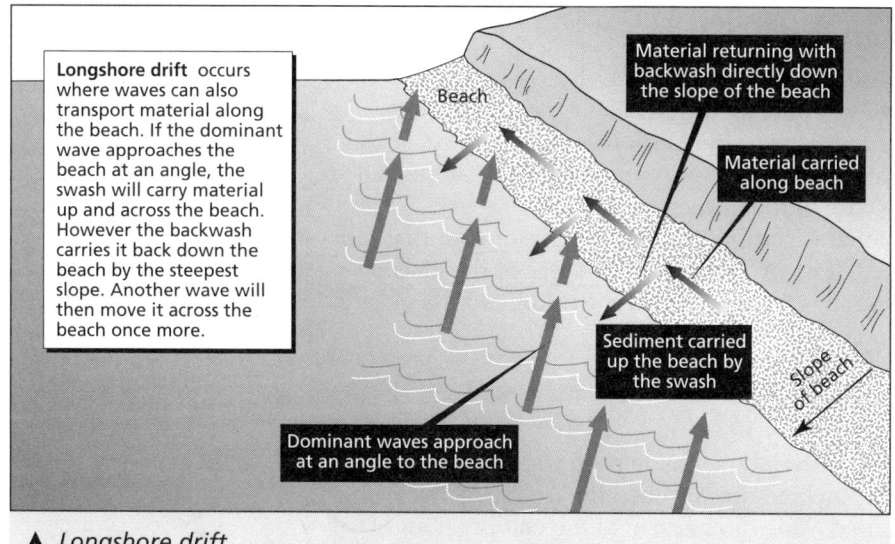

▲ Longshore drift

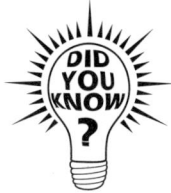

Beaches

The deposition of sediment results in the formation of beaches in sheltered bays. Beaches are nature's own answer to coastal protection. They absorb the energy released as waves break and they act as a buffer between the sea and the cliffs. There are two main sources of sediment:
- cliffs
- rivers.

Themes

Explain how waves transport sediment a) up and down a beach, and b) along the shore.

How does ice shape the landscape?

Key Idea
- Ice has the power to erode, transport and deposit material.

Key words and definitions

ice ages	Periods in which the polar ice sheets extended to lower latitudes covering large areas.
glaciers	Large rivers of ice that flow along valley bottoms.
moraine	The material transported by a glacier.
snout	The front end of a glacier.
corrie/cwm	Armchair-shaped hollow eroded into a mountainside by moving ice.

Glacial erosion

Glaciers erode the land in two ways:
1. **Plucking** Pressure causes the ice at the base of the glacier to melt. Meltwater seeps into cracks and joints and re-freezes. As the water freezes it expands, prising apart the rock and loosening large fragments.
2. **Abrasion** The fragments of rock transported by the glacier grind along the valley bottom and valley sides wearing away the rock.

How do glaciers transport material?

The material carried by a glacier is called **moraine**. Debris is frozen into the ice and carried along in the flow. There are three main types of moraine. They are classified according to where in the glacier they are carried.
- **Ground moraine** This material comes mainly from plucking at the valley floor and is carried at the base of the glacier.
- **Lateral moraine** This material is composed of fragments of rock that fall from the valley sides above. It is carried along the edges of the glacier.
- **Medial moraine** This material is transported in the middle of the glacier and is collected when two glaciers join together.

Glacial deposition

Glaciers eventually deposit the material they have been transporting. This deposition generally occurs in lowland areas. When the ice melts, the moraine can no longer be carried. This can happen at the end or snout of the glacier when the glacier is in retreat. Glacial moraine can also be spread over a much wider area.

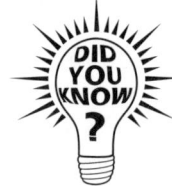

The last ice age ended approximately 10,000 years ago. During the ice age temperatures in northern Europe were much lower than they are now. The conditions were perfect for the formation of glaciers.

Hints and Tips!
Remember, in upland areas, glacial landforms are all associated with erosion.

Themes

Cover the page and see how many of these landforms you can remember.

Themes

Cover the page and list the three ways material is transported by a glacier.

The hydrological cycle

Key Ideas
- Water is continually circulating through a natural system of stores and transfers (transfers can be divided into inputs and outputs).
- The system can be studied at a global scale and river basin scale.
- People can modify the natural system by adding artificial stores and transfers.

Key words and definitions

Natural transfers (inputs and outputs)

evaporation	A transfer of water from the Earth's surface to the atmosphere where it changes from a liquid to gas.
condensation	A transfer of water vapour back into water droplets as a result of cooling.
transpiration	A transfer of water from vegetation to the atmosphere.
precipitation	Water transferred from the atmosphere to the Earth's surface as rain, snow and hail.
overland flow	Water transferred over the land's surface. This is the fastest route water can take to a river.
infiltration	Water moving vertically into the soil at its surface.
throughflow	Water moving sideways through air spaces in the soil. This is the second fastest route water can take to a river.
percolation	Water travelling vertically through the soil or rock.
groundwater flow	Water travelling sideways through permeable rock. This is the slowest route water can take to a river.
streamflow	The transfer of water in river channels.

Natural stores

oceanic stores	Water stored in the oceans.
atmospheric stores	Water in the atmosphere (stored as water vapour).
ice	Water stored as ice, e.g. at the poles and at the top of high mountains.
interception storage	Water stored on the leaves of trees.
depression storage	Water stored in depressions in the surface, e.g. puddles.
soil moisture	Water stored in air spaces in the soil.
groundwater	Water stored in air spaces in the rock.

Themes

Cover the page and see how many of these stores and transfers you can list in your notebook.

Hints and Tips!

Using the correct terms in your exam answers will gain you higher marks than describing the stores and transfers, and it can save you time!

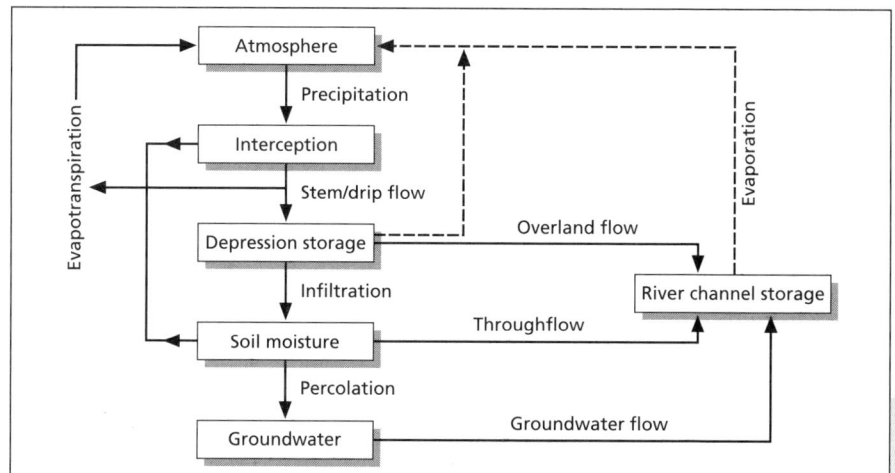

◀ *Systems diagram of the hydrological cycle*

Physical systems and environments

Drainage basins and hydrographs

Key Ideas
- Each **drainage basin** has a unique hydrological (flow of water) pattern affected by factors such as relief, vegetation, soil and rock type, and land use.
- The hydrology of a drainage basin will determine the **discharge** of a river.

Key words and definitions

confluence	The point where two rivers meet.
discharge	The volume of water in the river flowing past a certain point at a certain time.
drainage basin	The area drained by a river and its **tributaries**. This can also be called the catchment area.
impermeable	Surface that does not allow water to soak through.
lag time	The time between maximum rainfall during a storm and the peak flow in the river.
mouth	The point where a river meets the sea.
source	The point where a river begins.
tributary	A small river or stream feeding into a major river.
trunk stream	The main river in a drainage basin.
watershed	The division between two drainage basins.

Hints and Tips!
A drainage basin looks a little like a tree. The main river is the trunk, the tributaries are the branches. Practise drawing and labelling the features of a drainage basin in your notebook.

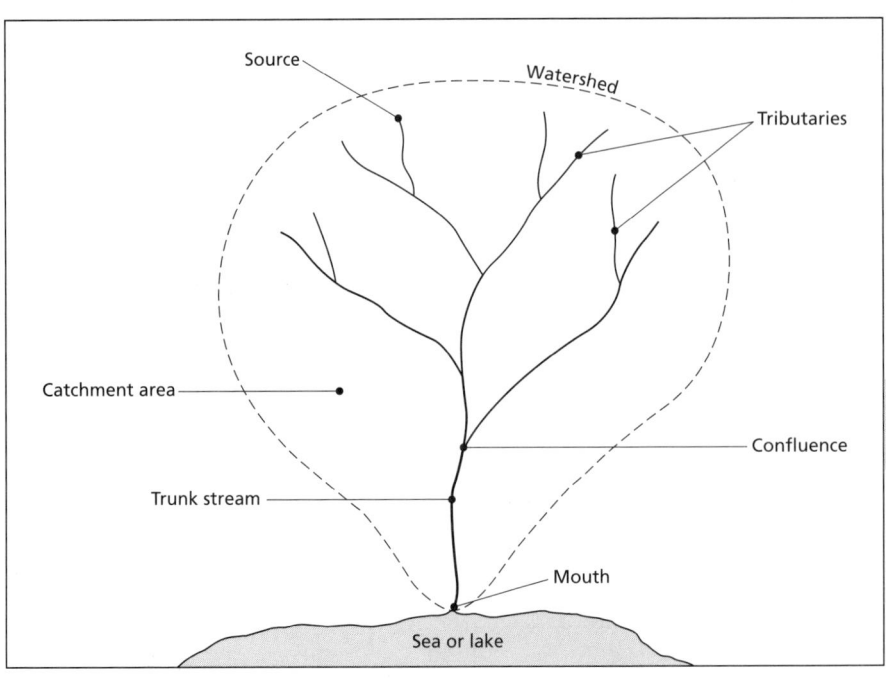

◀ *A typical drainage basin*

Hydrographs

A hydrograph shows the changes in discharge over time following a period of rainfall. The shape of the hydrograph will vary according to the amount and intensity of rainfall and the route taken to the river. Water will reach a river quickly if it travels as overland flow; it will take longer if water travels as throughflow or groundwater flow. A hydrograph shows:
- the duration and quantity of rainfall.
- the normal flow of the river.
- the rise and fall of discharge as a result of rainfall.
- the time between peak rainfall and peak discharge – **lag time**.

Hints and Tips!
To read a hydrograph effectively you need to be able to recognize these four features.

A flash response

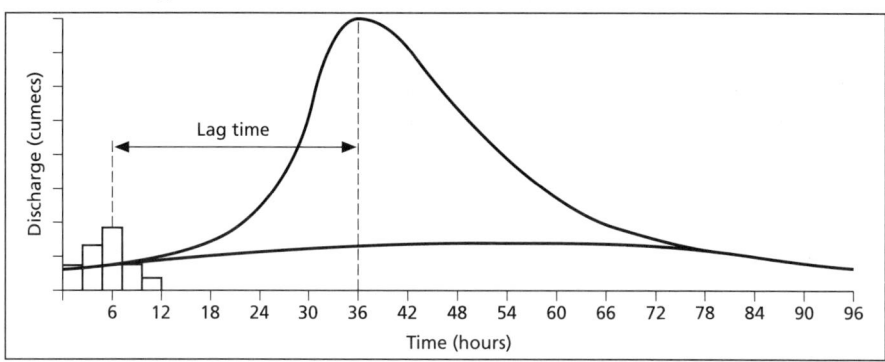

Flash response hydrograph

A flash response has a steep increase in **discharge**, a short **lag time**, and a high peak discharge. This type of graph suggests that rainfall is reaching the river quickly as overland flow rather than throughflow or groundwater flow. This pattern of water flow could be explained by:
- thin or saturated soils preventing **infiltration**
- impermeable rock preventing groundwater flow
- steep slopes preventing infiltration (water flowing too quickly to be absorbed)
- a lack of **interception** storage (little vegetation)
- urban land use creating impermeable surfaces and storm-drains
- high drainage density (lots of tributaries).

A flash response often leads to flooding because rainfall enters the river quickly causing river levels to rise sharply.

A lag response

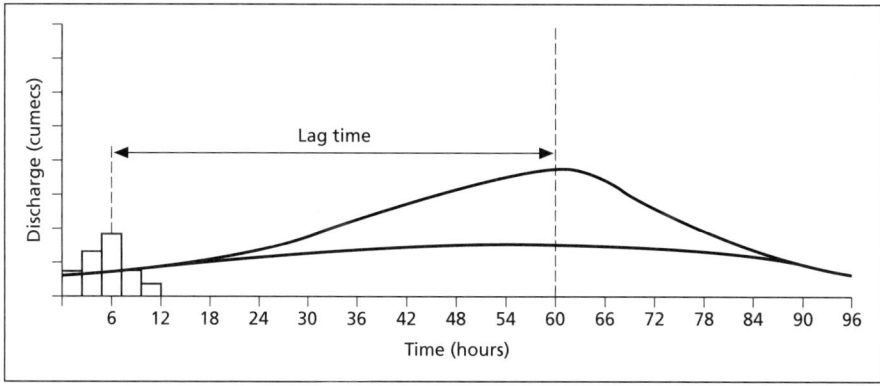

Lag response hydrograph

A lag response has a much slower rise in discharge, a longer lag time and a lower peak discharge. A graph of this nature suggests that water is reaching the river more slowly as throughflow or groundwater flow. This pattern of water flow could be explained by:
- deep soils which can absorb more rainfall
- permeable rock allowing water to travel as groundwater flow
- gentle slopes or flat land allowing water to infiltrate into the soil
- vegetation providing an interception layer
- low drainage density (few tributaries)
- storage reservoirs in upland areas.

Floods are rarely associated with hydrographs of this type because the rainfall reaches the river gradually over a long period of time.

Themes

Which of these factors will *not* result in a flash response: urban development, deforestation, dam construction, drainage of farmland?

How do rivers shape the landscape?

> **Key Idea**
> - Rivers have the power to erode, transport and deposit material.

Erosion

A river's power to erode depends on two factors:
- The velocity (speed) of the flow. The faster the flow the more energy a river has to erode the land.
- The discharge. High discharge allows a river to carry more material which in turn increases the rate of erosion.

River erosion involves four processes:
1. **Hydraulic action** The power of fast flowing water can tear material from the river channel.
2. **Corrosion** Water can dissolve certain minerals in the rock.
3. **Corrasion** The load carried by the river grinds away the river bed and banks.
4. **Attrition** Rocks carried by the river are gradually broken down into smaller pieces as they rub together.

Transportation

The material transported by a river is known as the **load**. A river's load is composed of dissolved material, small particles and giant rocks and boulders. Different types of particles are carried in different ways:
- **Traction** Large rocks and boulders (bedload) are dragged or rolled along the river bed.
- **Saltation** Smaller, lighter pebbles and gravel bounce along the river bed.
- **Suspension** Fine particles of silt and sand are suspended in the water giving it a cloudy appearance.
- **Solution** Some minerals will dissolve in the water.

Deposition

A river will deposit its load when it no longer has the energy to transport it. A river loses energy when it slows down on the inside of meanders or when it meets the sea. Limited deposition also occurs along the entire length of a river's course.

Themes

List and define the four processes of erosion and four of transportation associated with rivers.

Weather and climate

Key Ideas
- Climate is affected by latitude, relief, ocean currents and distance to the sea.
- Patterns of climate and weather can be identified at global, regional and local scales.

Key words and definitions
weather	The day-to-day changes in the state of the atmosphere.
climate	Average weather conditions over a long period of time.
microclimate	The weather conditions of a small area.
evapotranspiration	The return of water into the atmosphere as vapour.

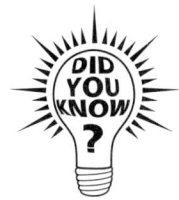

Temperatures in city centres can be over 5°C warmer than the surrounding suburbs!

Microclimate

What factors affect local weather conditions?
Local weather can be affected by a number of factors. These factors can affect local temperatures, wind conditions and precipitation.

Altitude
On average temperatures fall by 0.5°C for every 100m gained in altitude. Upland areas will generally be cooler than lowland areas as the air is thinner and wind speeds increase. Upland areas also experience high levels of precipitation as warm, moist air rises and cools over the mountains. This resulting condensation leads to relief rainfall.

Shelter
Sheltered areas tend to be warmer than more exposed areas as the cooling influence of the wind is reduced.

Aspect
South-facing places receive more sunshine than north-facing places. South-facing valley slopes tend to be warmer than north-facing slopes.

Vegetation
Evapotranspiration from vegetation increases humidity levels at a local scale. Vegetation can also deflect wind and so reduce wind speeds at ground level. The shelter offered by dense vegetation such as woodland can also lead to higher temperatures.

Water
Large bodies of water such as lakes and seas can have a moderating effect on surrounding areas. In summer air blowing over water is cooled as water does not heat up as fast as land. Breezes coming off the water will be cool. In winter water stays warm longer than land. Air blowing over water is warmed resulting in warm winds.

Urban areas
Concrete and tarmac absorb more of the sun's heat than trees or grass. Temperatures in urban areas are therefore higher in cities than in surrounding rural areas. This difference in temperatures is known as the urban heat island effect. Buildings can also deflect wind which creates localized areas of shelter, though they can increase wind speed elsewhere, e.g. streets forming wind tunnels.

Themes

Cover the page and try to list six factors affecting local weather or microclimates.

Hints and Tips!
As well as knowing the factors which affect microclimates, practise applying the ideas to real places. Using an OS map try to locate places affected by each of the six factors, e.g. a hilltop or a south-facing mountainside.

Regional climatic patterns in the British Isles

Key Ideas
- There are marked differences in climate across the British Isles.
- The climatic patterns of the British Isles are determined by latitude, relief, ocean currents, altitude, prevailing winds and the sea.

Key words and definitions
maritime climate   A climate moderated by being close to the sea; characterized by cool summers and mild winters.
isotherms   Lines joining points of the same temperature on a weather chart.
prevailing winds   The most common wind direction.

Temperature variations in the British Isles

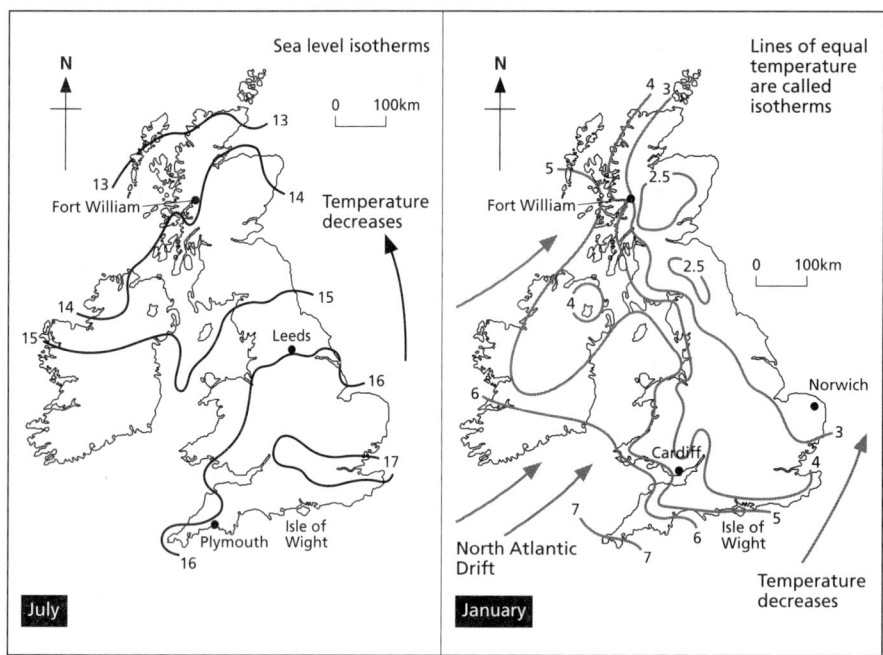

◀ *Temperature maps for the British Isles*

Pattern 1 In summer, temperatures are highest in the south east and decrease towards the north.

Explanation The variations in summer temperatures are associated with latitude. The sun is higher in the sky in the south than it is in the north. The sun's energy is more concentrated in the south resulting in higher temperatures. Further north the sun's energy is more spread out resulting in lower temperatures.

Pattern 2 In winter, temperatures are highest in the south west and decrease toward the north east.

Explanation In winter the western areas are warmed by the North Atlantic Drift, a warm ocean current which crosses the Atlantic bringing warm water from the Gulf of Mexico. The east of the British Isles is colder due to cold air from the continental landmass.

Precipitation
Pattern Precipitation is highest in western areas and decreases toward the east.

Explanation 1 The prevailing winds blow from the south west. Most rain-bearing weather fronts approach the British Isles from the west. Western areas therefore receive high levels of frontal rainfall.

Explanation 2 The west of the British Isles is more mountainous than the east. As warm moist air from the North Atlantic rises over the mountains it cools and condenses resulting in high levels of relief rainfall. The eastern regions fall within a rain shadow and receive much less rainfall.

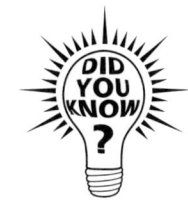

The wettest place in the UK is Fort William on the west coast of Scotland.

Global climatic patterns

Key Ideas
- The global climatic system is driven by the sun's energy.
- The interior of large continental land masses has a more extreme climate than coastal regions.
- Mountain ranges often have colder, wetter climates than the surrounding land mass.

Key words and definitions

low pressure (depressions)	Areas of warm, rising air which are associated with wind and rain.
high pressure (anticyclones)	Areas of cool, sinking air which are associated with clear skies and dry periods.
convection currents (in the atmosphere)	Flow of air as a result of the sun's heat.

Latitude
The variation in the amount of solar energy at different latitudes generates huge **convection currents** in the atmosphere. These convection currents result in areas of high and low pressure that have a significant influence over global climate patterns.

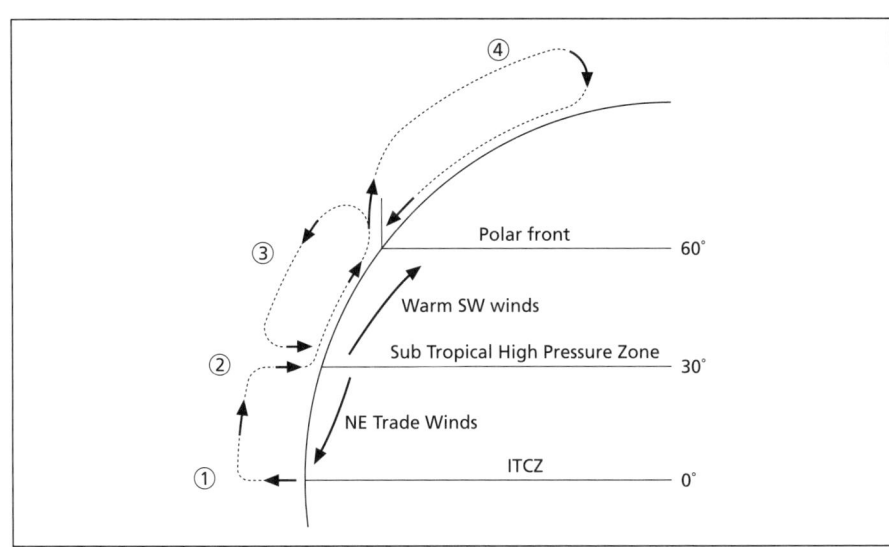

◀ *Global circulation patterns*

Areas of high and low pressure:
1. **The Inter Tropical Convergence Zone (ITCZ)**
   At the Equator the sun's energy is very intense resulting in high air temperatures. The warm air rises over the Equator creating an area of **low air pressure**. The warm air cools as it rises, condenses and produces high levels of convectional rainfall, characteristic of Equatorial regions.

The convection currents reach the upper atmosphere and migrate north and south.

2 **The Sub-Tropical High Pressure zone**
At around 30 degrees north and south of the Equator the air from the Equator has cooled and begins to sink back toward the surface creating bands of **high air pressure**. As the dry air sinks it becomes warmer resulting in hot desert regions. Warm air is sucked in to replace the rising air at the Equator creating the NE Trade Winds.

3 **The Polar Front**
At around 60 degrees north and south of the Equator warm tropical air collides with cold polar air. The warm air is forced up over the cold air creating areas of low air pressure. The low-pressure areas or depressions are responsible for the unsettled weather experienced in the British Isles. The rising air at the front pulls in air from the sub-tropics creating warm SW winds.

4 **The Polar Desert**
At high latitudes the sun's energy is spread thinly and air temperatures are low. Cold air sinks over the poles creating areas of high air pressure. The air is dry resulting in cold 'polar deserts'.

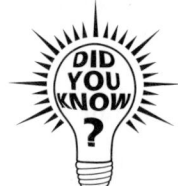

Sailors nicknamed the sub-tropical high-pressure zone the 'horse latitudes'. This was because ships caught in the hot, dry, windless regions had to throw their horses and livestock overboard to save water.

Three types of rainfall

Key Ideas
- All rainfall is caused when warm, moist air is forced to rise and cool resulting in **condensation** and ultimately rainfall.
- There are three main types of rainfall: relief rain, frontal rain and convection rain.

1 **Relief rain**
This occurs in mountainous areas where the prevailing winds blow warm, moist air up over the hills. As the air rises it is cooled and water vapour begins to condense back into water droplets. The result is high levels of rainfall in upland areas. As the air descends down the leeward (sheltered) side of the mountains the temperature rises again, condensation is reduced and the rain stops. As the descending air is drier the leeward side of mountains usually receives very little rainfall. These drier regions are said to fall within a *rain shadow*.

2 **Frontal rain**
A weather front is the point at which cold air and warm air collide. As warm air is lighter and less dense than cold air it rises up over the cold air. As it rises it cools, condenses and produces rain. At a warm front the warm air rises gently and slowly and this produces light but steady rainfall. At a cold front the cold air drives beneath the warm air forcing it to rise quickly, resulting in heavy downpours.

3 **Convection rain**
Convection rain occurs when the sun's heat warms the air at ground level. The warmed air rises and cools resulting in heavy rain. Convection rain is more common in the tropics where the sun is most intense. In Equatorial regions heavy downpours are produced most afternoons. Convection rain is also produced in higher latitudes in summer when the heat of the sun can trigger summer rain storms in the late afternoon.

Weather and climate

Weather associated with low-pressure systems

Key Idea
- There is a distinct weather pattern associated with the passing of a depression.

Key words and definitions
warm front Point where warm air rises over cold air.
cold front Point where cold air drives under warm air forcing it to rise.

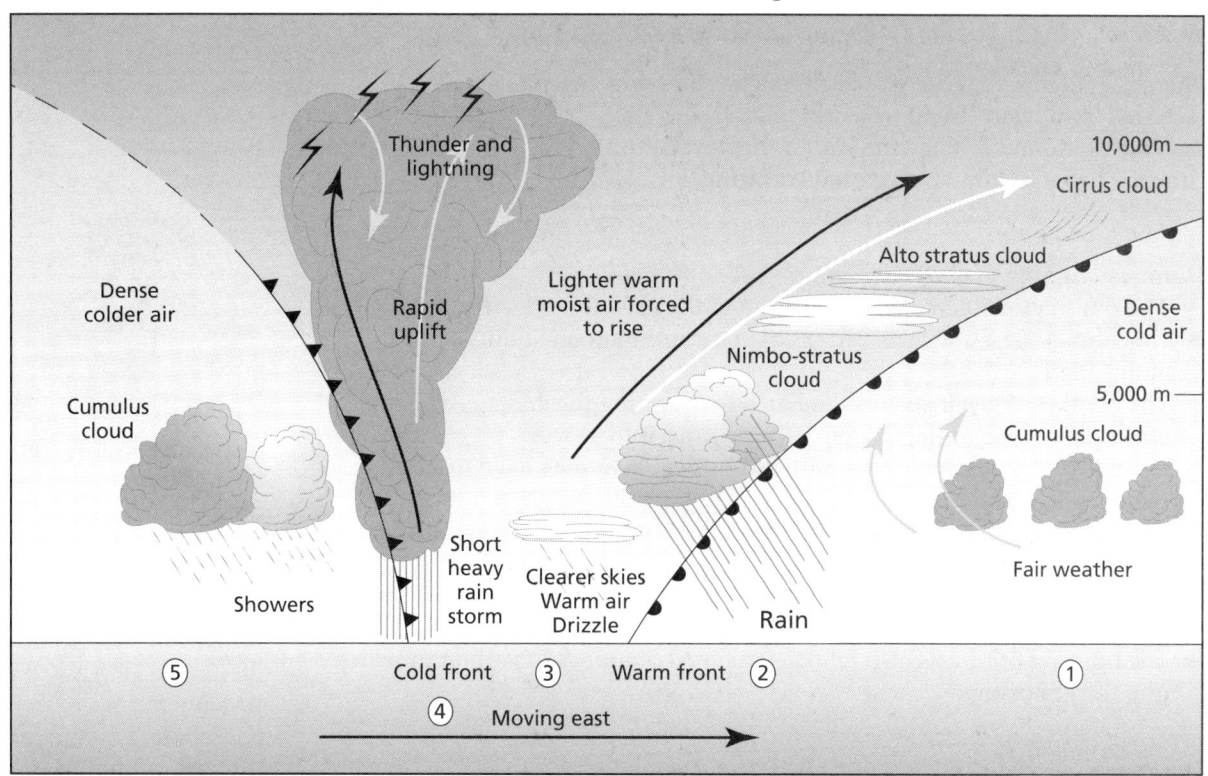

▲ *A depression*

Depressions develop over the North Atlantic where warm, moist air from the sub-tropics meets cold polar air. The pattern of weather that is produced can be divided into five clear stages. When interpreting the diagram above you must begin at the right-hand side and work toward the left.

Stage 1 A sector of cold air gives low temperatures. The cold air is heavy and sinks resulting in dry conditions. High cirrus cloud begins to form as the warm front approaches.

Stage 2 Light warm air collides with heavy cold air. As the two air masses do not mix the warm air rises gently over the cold air. As the warm, moist air rises it cools, condenses and forms nimbo-stratus rain clouds and steady rain follows.

Stage 3 As the warm front passes over temperatures will increase. The sky may clear for a short time and any rain turns to light drizzle.

Stage 4 At the cold front a sector of heavy cold air drives underneath the warm air forcing it to rise rapidly. The air cools as it rises and condenses quickly producing towering cumulo-nimbus clouds. Heavy downpours are common at the cold front. Temperatures fall as cold air approaches.

Stage 5 As the depression passes the heavy rain will ease giving way to showers and then sunny intervals until the next pressure system moves in from the North Atlantic.

Hints and Tips!
A depression is basically a 'warm air sandwich'. Two sectors of cold air gradually move together squeezing the warm air upward resulting in frontal rainfall and strong winds.

Climatic change

Key words and definitions

deforestation — Cutting down of forests.

global warming — The theory that world temperatures are rising due to human activities leading to excessive build up of carbon dioxide in the atmosphere, increasing the greenhouse effect.

greenhouse effect — Atmospheric gases act like a greenhouse preventing heat escaping out to space.

There is evidence that the global climate is changing. Scientists have recorded an upward trend in world temperatures and have predicted an increase of around 3° C by the end of the next century. This pattern of climate change is known as **global warming.**

What is causing global warming?
- The rise in global temperatures is due to the **greenhouse effect**.
- Greenhouse gases such as carbon dioxide and methane build up in the atmosphere.
- The blanket of gas insulates the Earth by trapping the sun's heat in the atmosphere, preventing it from escaping out into space.
- Greenhouse gases occur naturally but human activities have resulted in rising concentrations.
- The burning of fossil fuels has released more and more carbon dioxide into the atmosphere.
- Deforestation reduces nature's capacity to absorb the excess and convert it to oxygen through photosynthesis.
- The burning of forests also releases millions of tonnes of carbon dioxide into the atmosphere.

What are the consequences of global warming?
- Rising world temperatures may have far-reaching social and economic effects.
- The warmer temperatures will increase evaporation. Increased levels of water vapour in the atmosphere will contribute to further warming.
- There may be a 15 per cent increase in global cloud cover.
- The global circulation system may be disrupted resulting in a shift in the rain belts from the tropics to higher latitudes.
- The ice caps may melt causing global sea levels to rise. This may result in the flooding of low-lying regions such as Bangladesh.
- The number of extreme climatic hazards may increase.

What can be done to prevent climatic change?
- Reduce the use of fossil fuels by improving energy efficiency and developing alternative fuels and technology such as wind, solar and hydroelectricity.
- Support LEDCs in developing alternative sources of energy.
- Reduce the rates of global deforestation.

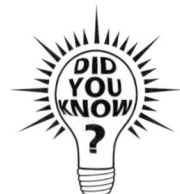

The MEDCs are responsible for 95 per cent of the increase in atmospheric carbon dioxide and if current rates continue the level of carbon dioxide will double by 2030. The LEDCs will become major contributors during the next century.

Climatic change

Living with global warming
As well as trying to reduce greenhouse emissions governments and planners must also prepare to adapt to climate change.
- We must assess areas at risk from flooding and invest in coastal protection schemes.
- We must commit resources to agricultural research, developing crops that will grow in arid and semi-arid regions.
- We must research and develop ways of coping with extreme climatic hazards.
- We must improve water supplies particularly in areas which will become much drier.

Places

Name four areas that are at risk from rising sea levels and describe the effects they may experience.

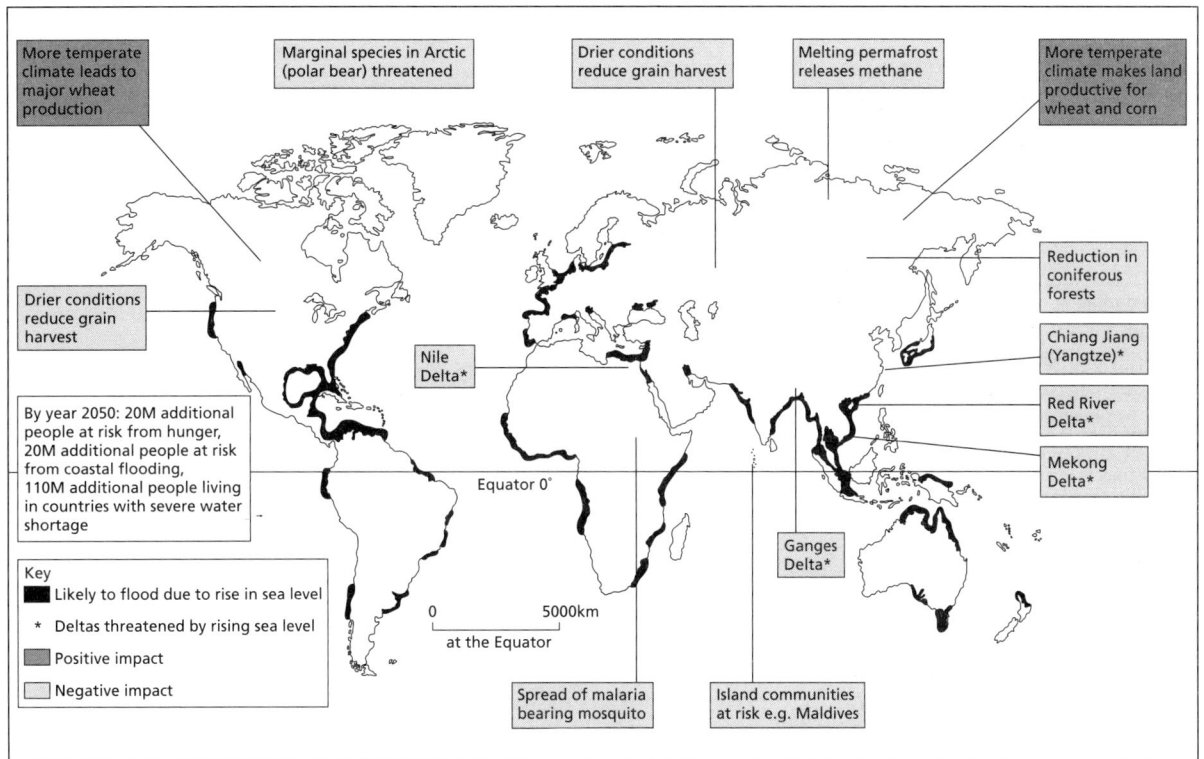

▲ Possible effects of global warming

Ecosystems: The Amazon Rainforest

Key Ideas
- Natural environments can be studied as systems
- There are complex links between climate, soils, vegetation and human activity in natural environments

Key words and definitions

deforestation	Cutting down of forests.
evapotranspiration	The return of water into the atmosphere as vapour.
convectional rainfall	Caused by the upward movement of warm moist air.
leaching	The removal of soil nutrients by water.
chemical weathering	Breakdown of rocks by chemical reactions, most involving rain water.
sedimentation	Build up of silt and sand.

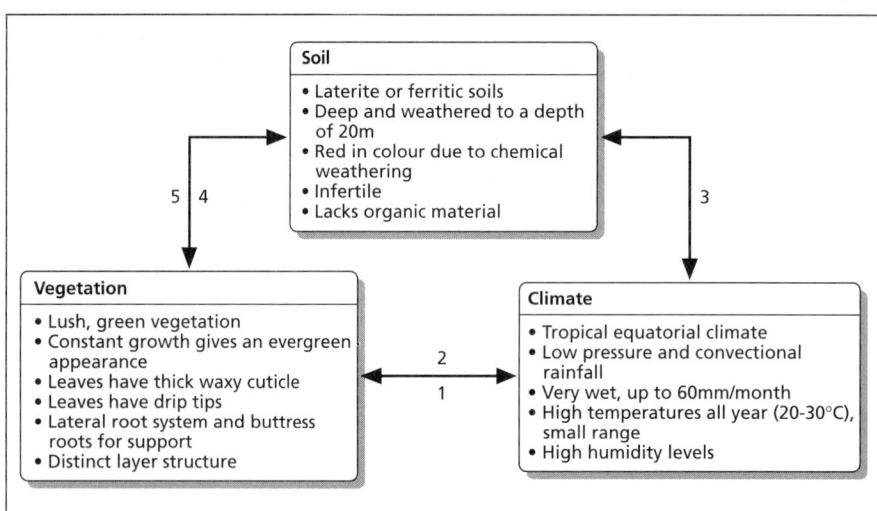

◀ Summary of equatorial environment

1 How climate affects the vegetation
- Constant high temperatures and rainfall produce a continual growing season that gives an 'evergreen' appearance to the rainforest. However the lack of seasons results in trees dropping leaves all year round.
- High temperatures result in rapid **evapotranspiration** and most plants have a thick, waxy cuticle to reduce water loss. Drip tips on leaves ensure water falls to the ground quickly where it can be absorbed by an efficient system of roots that criss-cross the forest floor, on or close to the surface.

2 How vegetation affects the climate
- Vegetation produces high levels of evapotranspiration resulting in high humidity levels. The water vapour in the atmosphere rises, cools and condenses resulting in high levels of **convectional rainfall**.

3 How climate affects the soil
- Heavy rainfall **leaches** nutrients from the soil resulting in infertility.
- High temperatures and moisture content result in rapid **chemical weathering** which produces deep, acidic soils high in iron and aluminium oxides.

4 How vegetation affects the soil
- Decomposition and the uptake of nutrients by the vegetation is so rapid that only small traces of nutrients remain in the soil.

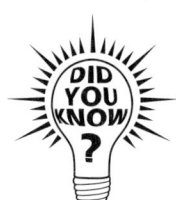

Every year an area of rainforest twice the size of Belgium is destroyed.

5 **How soil affects the vegetation**
- Vegetation has adapted to the infertile soils by developing a lateral root system close to the surface which absorbs the nutrients released by the decomposing litter layer before they leach out in the rainfall.

How can human activities affect a natural environment?

Know your case study

Deforestation in Amazonia

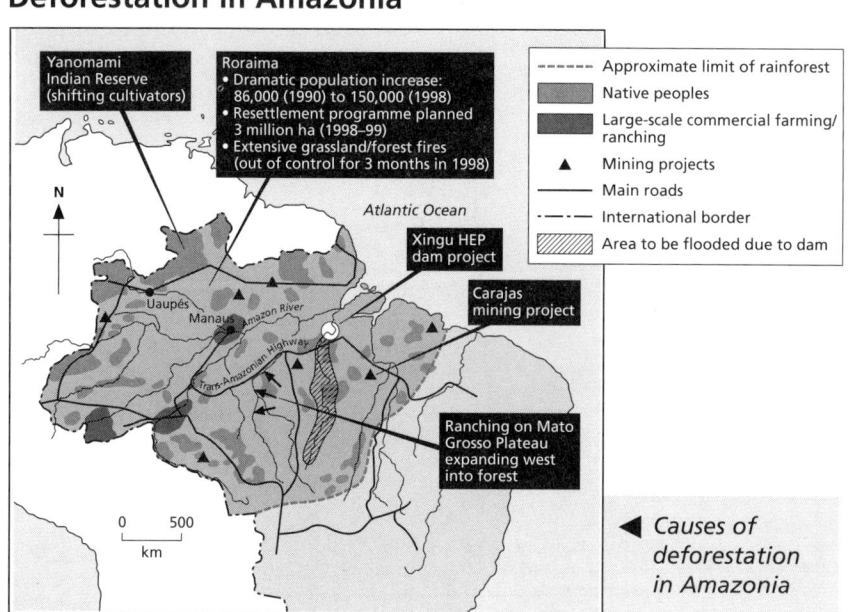

◀ Causes of deforestation in Amazonia

Causes of deforestation:
- government resettlement programmes and small-scale agriculture
- large-scale HEP developments
- large-scale mining
- ranching and large-scale agriculture
- communications and road building.

(For specific locations study the map above.)

Effects of deforestation on the soil:
- Removal of the **interception layer** (vegetation) increases leaching of nutrients and also surface run-off which causes soil erosion. Loss of soil can result in **sedimentation** of rivers, bank erosion and localized flooding. Aquatic life may die as sediment prevents the penetration of sunlight reducing photosynthesis and deoxygenating the water.

Effects of deforestation on the climate:
- Removal of vegetation reduces the rate of evapotranspiration and leads to falling humidity levels. This can lower rainfall and produce drier conditions.

Effects of deforestation on vegetation:
- The dry conditions can increase the risk of fire that can destroy large sections of forest.
- The lush vegetation of the rainforest is replaced by secondary forest or grassland. The diversity of species is reduced and many may become extinct.

Hints and Tips!

Environmental issues often arouse strong emotions. You must try to remain objective when discussing them and not give an over-emotional response.

Hints and Tips!

Although deforestation is an important issue, over 80 per cent of the Amazon rainforest is untouched. We must also look at the reasons for deforestation. Brazil can increase GDP by clearing the rainforest for farming, dams and mining. Higher GDP will lead to economic and social development and higher standards of living.

Places

1. Give four examples of developments in Brazil or another LEDC that caused deforestation or other environmental damage.

2. Describe the effects that your chosen development has on the soil, climate and vegetation.

Exam practice – foundation level paper

This question is about Physical Systems and Environments.

Study grid squares 9623 and 9923 on the map of Cheltenham on page 107.

(a) (i) Which grid square will have the higher **rainfall**?
    (ii) Give one reason for your answer. [2]

(b) (i) Which grid square will have the higher **temperatures**?
    (ii) Give one reason for your answer. [2]

(c) Study these graphs.

▶ *Delaware River, New York State, 1975*

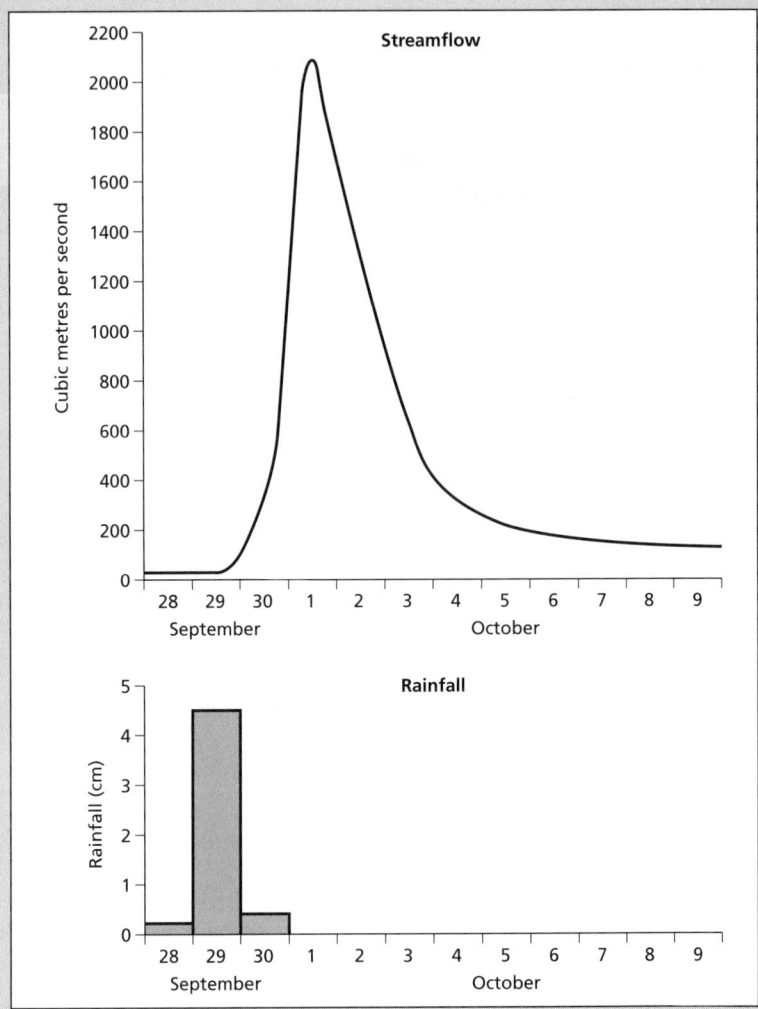

    (i) On which dates did the **peak rainfall** and the **peak streamflow** happen?
    (ii) Explain the difference in the timing of the two peaks. [4]

(d) Suggest one reason why
    (i) the flow in the river was very low before the rain fell
    (ii) the flow did not drop quickly back to the level it was before the rain fell. [4]

(e) Choose an area where you have studied the climate and vegetation.
    (i) Name and locate the area.
    (ii) Describe its climate and vegetation.
    (iii) Explain how people's activities in the area are changing the environment. [5]

Check your answers at the back of the book. [Total 20 marks]

Ecosystems: The Amazon Rainforest

Exam practice – higher level paper

B4 This question is about Physical Systems and Environments. It is taken from the 1998 Higher Paper.

Study the OS map extract on page 107.

(a) Describe two differences you would expect to find in the weather in winter between grid squares 9623 and 9923. [2]

(b) Give a reason for each of the differences you mentioned in (a). [2]

Study the weather map shown below.

(c) Describe and explain the weather at the station in south-west Ireland. [4]

(d) How might the weather in the south of England have changed during the 24 hours after the map was drawn? [4]

(e) Many physical environments are under threat.
  (i) Name and describe the location of a physical environment.
  (ii) Describe the links between its climate and vegetation.
  (iii) Explain why your chosen environment might be under threat. [8]

Check your answers at the back of the book.

[Total 20 marks]

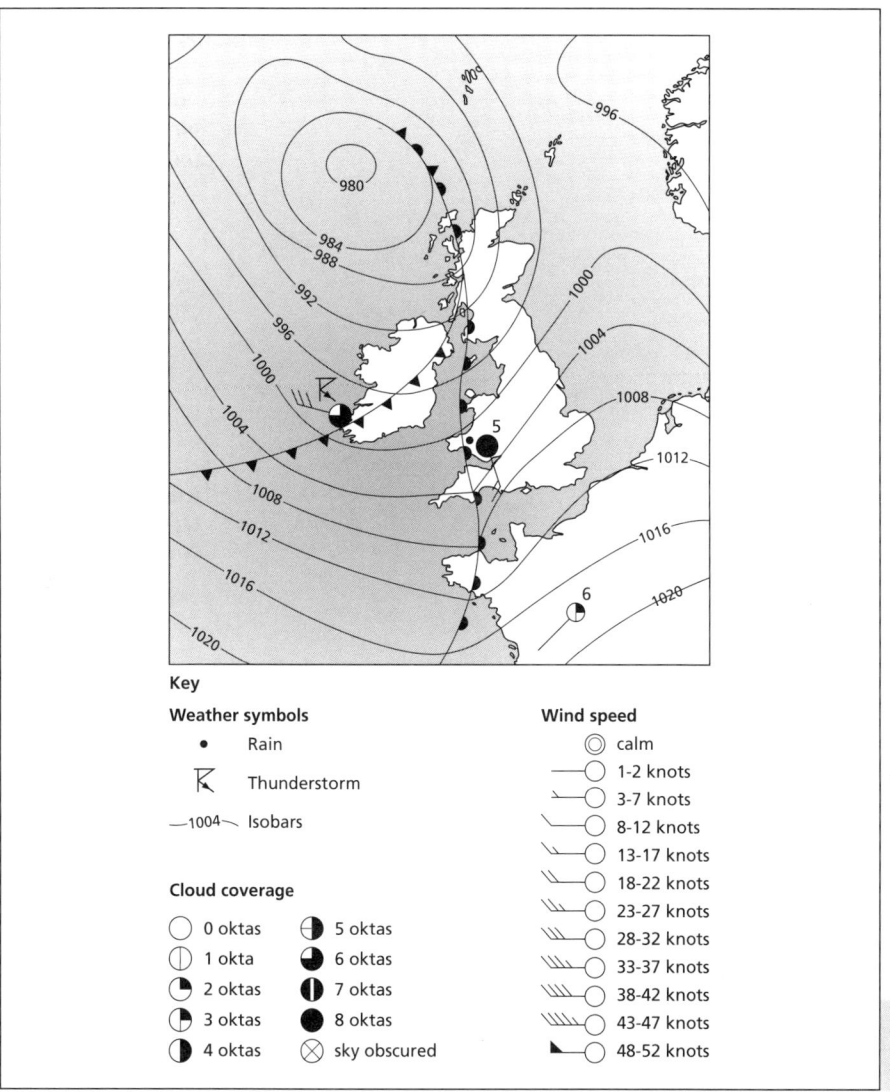

A weather map of the British Isles

Summary

Physical systems and environments

Theme 1 check list

	Confident	Not bad	Needs more work
Processes operating on the landscape			
I know the main types of weathering	☐	☐	☐
I know how the sea erodes, transports and deposits material	☑	☐	☐
I know how glaciers erode, transport and deposit material	☐	☐	☐
I know how rivers erode, transport and deposit material	☑	☐	☐
Physical environments and systems			
I know the components of the hydrological cycle	☑	☐	☐
I know the features of a drainage basin system – inputs, flows, stores and outputs	☑	☐	☐
I can intepret a hydrograph	☐	☐	☐
I know the links between climate, soil, vegetation and human activity in an environment	☑	☐	☐
Atmospheric processes and climate			
I know the factors that affect microclimates	☐	☐	☐
I know the factors affecting climate in different parts of the British Isles	☐	☐	☐
I know how the weather of the British Isles is affected by depressions and anticyclones	☐	☐	☐
I know how latitude, land and sea, relief and ocean currents affect the global pattern of climate	☐	☐	☐
I know possible reasons for global climate change	☐	☐	☐
I know possible effects of global climatic change	☐	☐	☐

Test Yourself

Tick the boxes – if you still do not understand seek help from your teacher.

Hints and Tips!

Write down the names of your chosen case studies. Ask your teacher to check your choices.

Know your case studies

Which real places have you studied as an example of:
- Local microclimate — name and location _____
- the climate in different parts of the British Isles — name and location _____
- one other contrasting climate from elsewhere in the world (it can be either from an MEDC or an LEDC) — name and location _____
- the links between people and an ecosystem — name and location _____

Theme 2: Natural hazards and people

For this theme you will need to know about:
- the nature and distribution of natural hazards
- the processes responsible for natural hazards
- the effects of natural hazards on people and places

This section will help you to revise your work on natural hazards. In the exam you may be set questions on any or all of the following:
1. What different kinds of natural hazard are there?
2. Where and why do different kinds of natural hazards occur?
3. What are the processes responsible for natural hazards?
4. How can people's activities affect natural hazards?
5. Do natural hazards affect people in LEDCs and MEDCs in the same way?
6. How can people predict, prevent and control natural hazards?

Hints and Tips!
A flood which does not adversely affect human life or activities is not a hazard, just a natural process.

Key words and definitions

risk	The potential danger or damage created by an event or phenomenon
short term	A hazard lasting for a short period (less than a day)
medium term	A hazard that lasts for a few weeks
long term	A hazard that lasts for over a month
tectonic	Associated with the movement of the tectonic plates in the Earth's crust
disaster	An event that has a negative impact on human life and activities

What is a natural hazard?

This is a question we must answer before we go any further. A hazard is a phenomenon or event which is seen to be a risk to human life or activities. A natural hazard is simply a danger or threat caused by natural processes such as tectonic activity or climatic change.

There are many different kinds of natural hazards. Some occur very rarely, some occur more frequently. Some hazards may last for a short time; some hazards last for a very long period of time. Some hazards affect only a localized area; some can affect the whole planet.

Tectonic hazards: earthquakes and volcanoes

Key words and definitions

albedo effect	Reflection of the sun's rays by particles in the atmosphere.
continental crust	Crust which makes up the continents is between 25 and 90km thick. It is less dense than oceanic crust and floats on top of the mantle.
convection currents	Currents created by the core's heat cause the molten rock in the mantle to circulate. This circulation is responsible for the movement of the crustal plates.
core	The centre of the Earth which consists of heavy metal deposits and which is extremely hot. The extreme pressure on the core means that the core is solid.
earthquake	The shaking of the Earth's crust as a result of plate movements.
lahars	Volcanic mud slides
lava	Molten rock which is erupted from a volcano.
magma	The molten rock in the mantle.
mantle	A layer of molten rock or magma which lies between the crust and the core.
oceanic crust	Crust beneath the oceans. This crust is mainly basalt and is incredibly heavy and dense.
plate boundary	The point at which two plates meet.
pyroclastic flow	High speed flow of hot gases and rocks.
seismometer	Machine that measures earth tremors.
subduction	The sinking of an oceanic plate beneath a lighter continental plate at a destructive plate boundary (see page 40 for descriptions of boundaries).
tectonic plates	The huge fragments which make up the Earth's crust.
volcano	A cone-shaped mountain formed from ash and lava which erupts from the mantle along plate boundaries.

Hints and Tips!
Ask somebody to test you on these key terms to ensure you know them all.

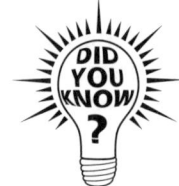

All the continents were once part of a giant landmass called Pangaea. This super-continent gradually drifted apart due to the convection currents in the mantle.

Plate tectonics

The Earth's crust is made up of large fragments called plates. These float on the surface of the **mantle**. The mantle is a layer of molten rock which is heated by the core. The heat creates **convection currents** that cause the molten rock to move. The movement within the mantle causes the plates to move around on the surface.

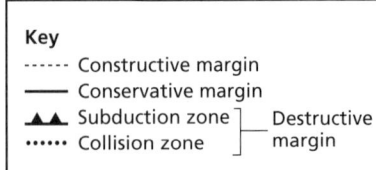

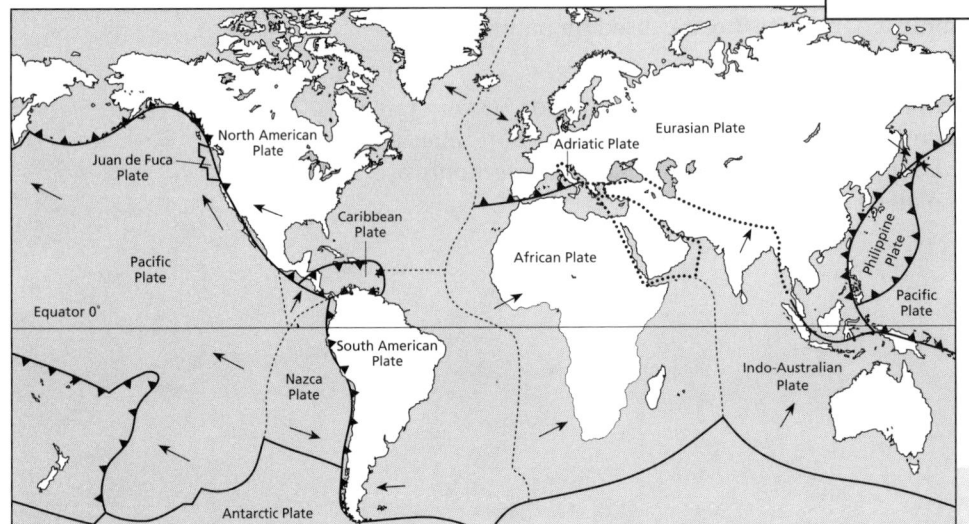

◀ *Global plates*

Tectonic hazards: earthquakes and volcanoes

Diagram	Movement	Example	Features
Constructive	Two plates moving apart (usually oceanic)	South American and African Plate moving apart in the mid-Atlantic Ocean	• New crust is formed - volcanic islands • Oceanic ridges develop, e.g. mid-Atlantic ridge • Earthquakes • Gentle volcanic activity
Destructive	An oceanic plate and continental plate moving towards each other	The Nazca Plate and the South American Plate colliding along west coast of South America	• Oceanic crust is destroyed as it sinks into the mantle • Deep oceanic trenches form off the continent • Fold mountains are created as crust is crumpled upwards by force of the collision • Earthquakes occur due to build up of friction • Volcanoes are created by build up of pressure in the mantle
Conservative	Two plates either sliding past each other in opposite directions or sliding alongside each other at different speeds	The Pacific Plate and North American Plate in California, USA	• Crust is neither created nor destroyed • Violent earthquakes occur due to build up of friction
Collision	Two continental plates colliding	The Eurasian Plate and the Indian Plate colliding as the Indian Plate moves northwards	• Fold mountains, such as the Himalayas, are formed • Violent earthquakes occur as the crust is thrust upwards

▲ *Plate boundaries*

Natural hazards and people

Plates move in three different ways:
1 Some plates move towards each other
2 Some plates move apart
3 Some slide past each other.

Plate boundaries

Geographers have identified four types of plate boundary (see page 31).

Where do tectonic hazards occur?

Volcanoes
▲ Volcanoes usually occur in long narrow belts.
▲ Volcanoes occur along destructive and constructive plate boundaries and at hot spots.
▲ Volcanoes occur frequently along the Pacific ring of fire (boundary of the Pacific plate).
▲ Volcanoes do occasionally occur away from plate boundaries.

Hints and Tips!
Hot spots generally are on constructive plate boundaries

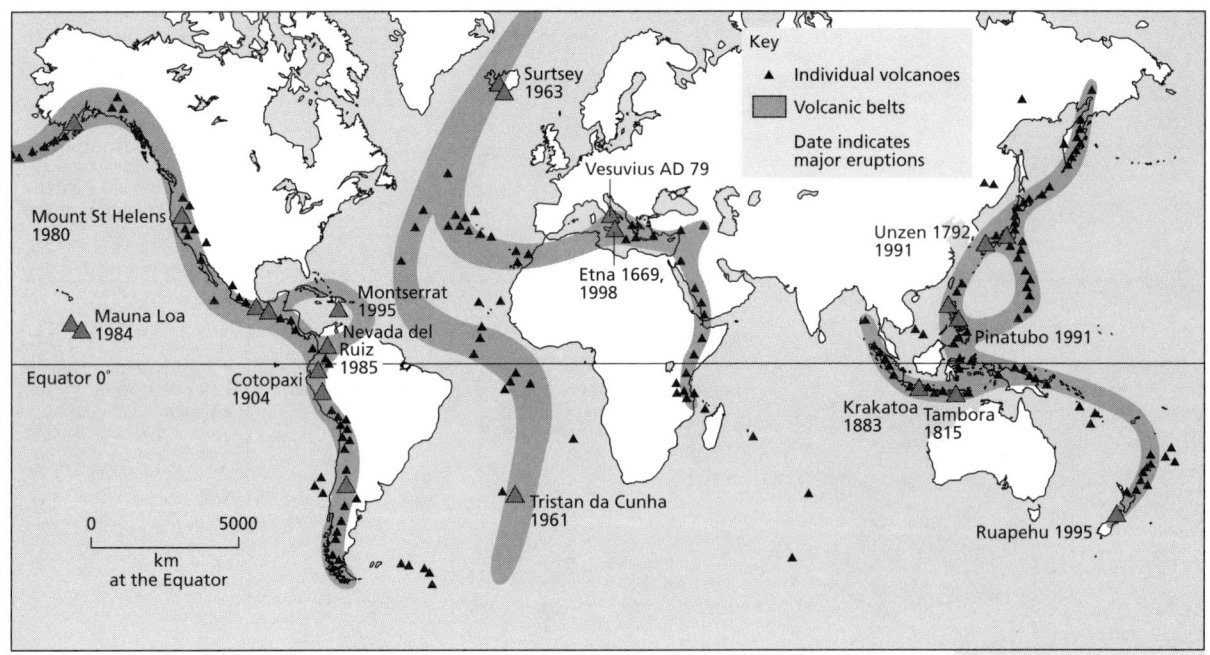

▲ Distribution of volcanoes

Causes of tectonic hazards

Volcanic eruptions occur as a result of a chain of events. The causes are different at the different types of plate boundary and at hot spots. At a destructive plate boundary volcanic eruptions occur because:
1 An oceanic plate subducts or sinks beneath a lighter continental plate.
2 The heat of the mantle melts and destroys the oceanic plate.
3 The newly created molten rock creates pressure in the mantle.
4 The pressure forces magma to the surface through weaknesses in the crust.
5 **Lava** erupts through the crust creating a volcano and reducing the pressure in the mantle below.

A similar chain of events can lead to earthquakes at destructive plate boundaries:
1 Movement of plates creates stress and friction as the crust bends.
2 Stress and friction builds up deep within the crust.

Hints and Tips!
Try to identify the patterns of volcanoes and earthquakes on the maps on pages 32 and 33.

Tectonic hazards: earthquakes and volcanoes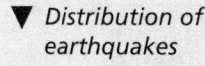

3 Stress and pressure are released as the crust snaps back into place.
4 The rapid movement of the crust sends shock waves radiating outwards from the point of origin called the focus.
5 When the shock waves reach the surface they cause the ground to shake.

Earthquakes and volcanoes also occur at other plate boundaries (see page 31) where the causes are different.

▼ *Distribution of earthquakes*

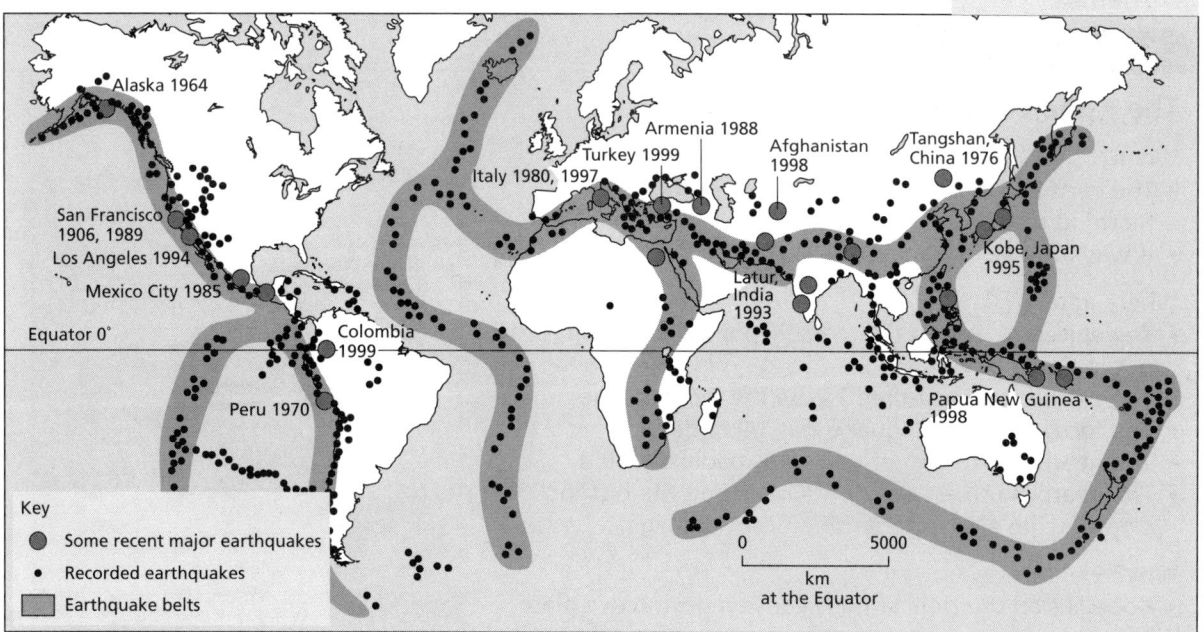

Earthquakes
- Earthquakes occur in three long narrow belts: a) around the Pacific plate, b) along the Mid-Atlantic Ridge and c) the southern boundary of the Eurasian plate.
- Earthquakes occur along all types of plate boundary.
- Earthquakes occur beneath land and sea.
- Earthquakes seldom occur away from plate boundaries.

Why are some earthquakes more serious than others?

It is not just the size of an earthquake which affects the seriousness of the disaster. It is often where it occurs that will determine the level of damage:
- The level of development will affect a country's ability to prepare for earthquakes and cope with the aftermath. For instance Mexico cannot afford the high-tech solutions used in Japan.
- An earthquake with an epicentre close to densely populated urban centres will cause more damage and risk to human life than one in a sparsely populated rural district.
- The type of rock the waves pass through is also important. Firm bedrock such as granite can withstand the stress but shale and silt will make the shaking worse.

Hints and Tips!
Try to memorize the five stages for both volcanoes and earthquakes to give a good clear explanation in the exam.

Themes
Use the table on page 31 and your own notes to explain why earthquakes and volcanoes occur at constructive, conservative and collision boundaries.

Hints and Tips!
Think of five effects which would occur in an urban area which would not occur in a rural area.

Natural hazards and people

Test Yourself Themes

Complete the paragraph below.

Volcanoes are created at destructive plate boundaries when a heavy _____ plate _____ beneath a lighter _____ plate. The heat of the _____ destroys the oceanic plate, which becomes molten. The _____ builds up in the mantle forcing molten rock upward through weaknesses in the _____. If the magma reaches the surface a _____ is formed.

Know your case study

The Kobe Earthquake

When?
- The earthquake struck at 5.46am just before the morning rush hour.
- It was Tuesday, 17 January 1995.

Where and how?
- The epicentre was on the sparsely populated Awaji island out in Osaka Bay.
- The earthquake measured 7.2 on the Richter scale.
- The focus of the earthquake was 14km deep.
- The nearby port town of Kobe was badly affected.
- The nearby business centre of Osaka and the historic centre Kyoto also suffered significant damage.

Why?
- Kobe lies on the Nojima fault above a destructive plate boundary.
- The oceanic Pacific and Philippine Plates are subducting (sinking) beneath the continental Eurasian Plate at a rate of 6.8cm a year.
- The stress created by this movement was suddenly released sending shockwaves along the fault line.

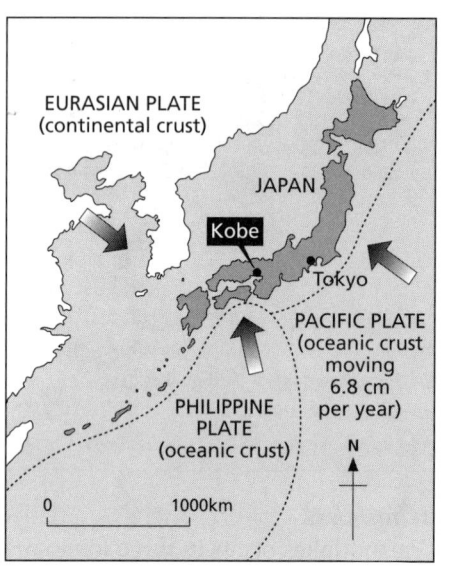

What happened?
The effects of an earthquake can be divided into primary and secondary effects. But you should also be aware that there are social, economic and physical effects.

Primary effects:
- 5,477 people were killed.
- 316,000 people were made homeless.
- 12 trains were derailed.
- The eastern line of the bullet train buckled.
- Part of the elevated Hanshin Expressway collapsed.
- The port facilities were destroyed
- Water and gas mains ruptured cutting off supply to one million homes.

Secondary effects:
- Over 200 people were crushed in their vehicles beneath the Hanshin Expressway.
- Fires spread as a result of ruptured gas mains.
- Thousands of businesses were forced to close.
- Trade in and out of the port was seriously affected.
- The total cost was estimated to be 10 billion Yen.

What help was given?
- 316,000 people were given emergency accommodation in public buildings.
- Meals and bottled water were flown in.
- The Japanese army co-ordinated rescue efforts.

Tectonic hazards: earthquakes and volcanoes

Know your case study

The Mount Pinatubo volcanic eruption

When?
- The volcano began to erupt on Sunday, 9 June 1991 at 6am.
- On 12 June three major eruptions occurred.
- Another major eruption occurred on 14 June.

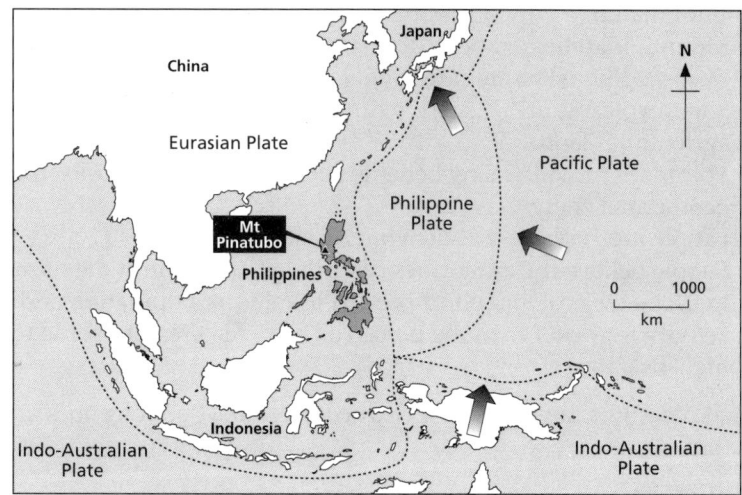

Where?
- Mount Pinatubo (Mt Mayan) is on the island of Luzon in the Philippines.
- The volcano is 100km north west of the capital city Manila.
- The Clark USAF base was located 10km to the east.

Why?
- The volcano lies on a destructive plate boundary.
- The oceanic Philippine Plate is subducting (sinking) under the continental Eurasian Plate.
- Pressure was building up within the mantle until magma was forced upwards into the magma chamber.
- A blockage in the volcano vent caused a build up of gases which resulted in massive explosions.

What happened?
It is best to consider the effects of a volcanic eruption as short-term and long-term impacts.

Short-term effects
- 400 earthquakes were felt in 24 hours immediately prior to the major eruption on 12 June.
- 20 million tonnes of sulphur dioxide were released into the stratosphere.
- The explosions sent ash and pumice to a height of 25km.
- Only six people died as a result of the explosions. 1500 died in the aftermath.
- **Pyroclastic flows** (ash and other debris) cascaded down river valleys at 80 km/h destroying everything in their path and disrupting drainage patterns, e.g. Pasig valley, which was completely filled in.
- Ash fell over a 600km radius turning day into night.
- Typhoon Yunya passed to the north of Luzon on 15 June. Tropical rains turned ash into mud triggering **lahars**.
- Lahars devastated the 1991 rice harvest.
- Water was contaminated and irrigation systems destroyed.
- 200,000 buildings were destroyed
- 650,000 people lost their jobs.
- 50,000 people were made homeless.
- 1 million farm animals are estimated to have been killed.

Long-term effects
- Mud and ash deposits prevented planting of the 1992 rice crop.
- Lahar activity will probably continue until 2001.
- Ash and gas clouds circled the Earth and scientists have noted an increased **albedo effect** (reflected light) and a fall in global temperatures of 1°C.
- Chlorine gas was thought to be responsible for a thinning of the ozone layer.
- The US airforce decided to close their base on Luzon.

Living with earthquakes and volcanoes

As these examples show living in areas prone to volcanic eruptions or earthquakes is very dangerous. Why did 15,000 people live on the slopes of Mount Pinatubo? Why do people continue to live in Kobe?

- Mount Pinatubo had been dormant for 600 years. Volcanic eruptions and major earthquakes are rare events.
- Soil in volcanic areas is fertile due to ash fall and creates productive agricultural land.
- Volcanoes provide many benefits such as mineral deposits, tourism, and geothermal energy.
- People are very good at denying a risk exists.
- People believe the authorities can predict and control the hazards.
- Inertia – the cost and effort needed to relocate population and economic activity is greater than the perceived risk. As a result people remain in high-risk areas.

What measures can be taken to reduce the impact of volcanoes and earthquakes?

Prediction

Volcanoes can be monitored for a number of warning signs which can be used to predict an eruption.

1. Shallow earthquakes indicate magma shifting beneath the ground.
2. Tiltmeters monitor changes in the slope.
3. Lasers detect minute changes in the ground surface.
4. Temperatures within the ground may increase.
5. Water levels in wells often fall.
6. Emissions of volcanic gases tend to increase.
7. Animals behave erratically.

Earthquakes are more difficult to predict and as yet no reliable method exists. Research is being undertaken into electrical conductivity and remote sensing, animal behaviour and even the claims that some people possess the power to predict earthquakes.

Measuring earthquakes

Seismometers are buried in the ground and detect vibrations beneath the surface. These readings are transmitted to a seismograph, which draws a trace of the shockwaves as they pass. Scientists can then estimate the size of the earthquake and the level of damage likely to result from it.

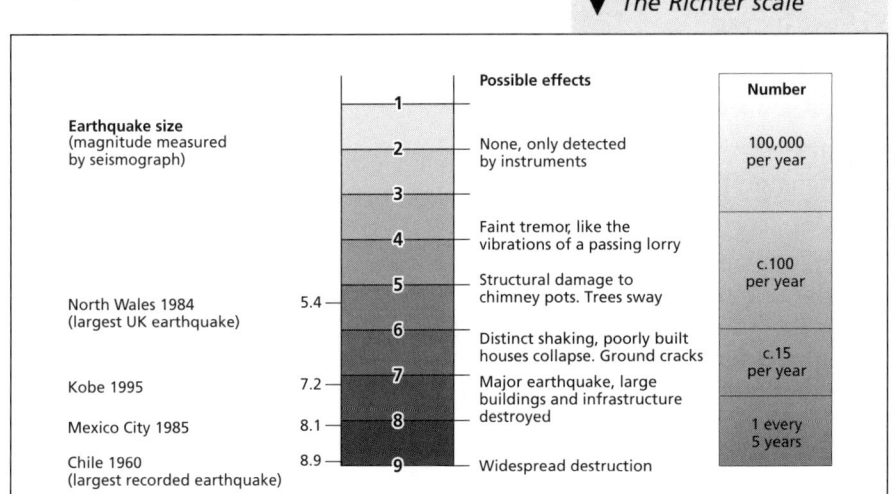

▼ The Richter scale

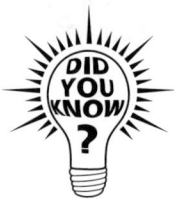

Plumes of steam and gas were given off by Mount Pinatubo in the Spring of 1991. Monitoring these and the seismic activity the US Geological Survey issued a warning on 2 June allowing 120,000 people to be evacuated safely. Unfortunately some people were left behind who were still within the disaster zone.

Places

You may have studied other volcanic eruptions such as Mt. St. Helens or Montserrat. Can you identify any similarities or differences between two eruptions in MEDCs and LEDCs?

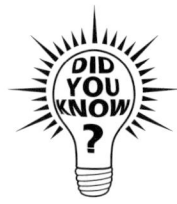

Every month Tokyo experiences three noticeable earthquakes!

Tectonic hazards: earthquakes and volcanoes

The size of earthquakes is measured on a 9-point scale called the Richter scale. This scale is a logarithmic scale so a quake at level 2 is ten times the size of a level 1 quake.

Protection and preparation

Most people recognize that preparation can be as effective at reducing the impact of earthquakes and volcanic eruptions as accurate prediction.

Japan leads the world in earthquake protection:
1. Japan has a public education programme which instructs people how to act in the event of an earthquake. Every year on the anniversary of the great Kanto earthquake an earthquake drill is held to practise emergency procedures.
2. Households have emergency kits including bottled water, food rations, first aid kits, warm blankets, a fire extinguisher and a radio.
3. Water tanks are located throughout the city to provide up to 10 days' emergency supply should water pipes break.
4. Parks are designed to provide refuge from falling objects.
5. High-rise buildings are constructed in a box-like way so that one storey may collapse leaving the others standing.
6. Heavy furniture is bolted to the walls to prevent it toppling over.
7. Foundations are anchored deep into the bedrock with rubber shock absorbers installed.
8. Many private homes have been replaced using less flammable materials.
9. Flexible gas and water mains are used in some parts of the city.
10. Since 1981 all new buildings have to be earthquake-proof.%

> **Hints and Tips!**
> Make a note of any questions you feel unsure of and check back in the text and your notes and textbook or ask your teacher for advice.

Test Yourself — Themes

1. What are tectonic plates?
2. Why do plates move around?
3. Name the four types of plate boundary.
4. Name two hazards associated with plate boundaries.
5. Draw a flow diagram showing the five steps leading to volcanic eruptions at destructive plate boundaries.
6. Give four ways people can predict a volcanic eruption.
7. List five things people living in earthquake zones can do to protect themselves and reduce the impact of a disaster.
8. Using your own notes and textbook, explain (using examples) why LEDCs find it more difficult to cope with disasters such as earthquakes.

Test Yourself — Places

1. For an MEDC that has suffered from an earthquake, explain why the disaster happened, and give four ways that the place was affected by the eathquake.
2. For an LEDC that you have studied, describe the effects earthquakes have had on the population and economic activity.
3. Name a place you have studied that has suffered from a volcanic eruption. List four causes and four effects of the disaster.

Floods

Floods occur when the discharge (the amount of water flowing through the river) is more than what the channel can hold. Some rivers are more likely to flood than others. There are a number of factors that make a flood more likely. Some of them are natural; some of them are affected by human activities. They include:

- **A high drainage density** A river with many **tributaries** will drain water more quickly.
- **Deforestation** The removal of the **interception layer** (vegetation) will increase overland flow.
- **Urbanization** Impermeable surfaces such as concrete generates more overland flow.
- **Steep slopes** Rain falling on steep slopes cannot **infiltrate** (soak through) and will reach the river very quickly.
- **Thin soils** Thin soils become saturated very quickly.
- **Impermeable rock** If underlying rock is **impermeable** overland flow will be greatest.
- **Meanders** As a river meanders the speed of flow is forced to slow down sometimes causing the water level to rise.
- **Drainage** Agricultural land is often drained to improve productivity, reducing the lag time and increasing the risk of flooding.
- **Extreme climatic conditions** Intense rain storms or long period of continual rainfall may cause flooding.

Know your case study

The 1993 Mississippi Flood

When?
- August 1993

Where?
- An area of approximately 8 million hectares stretching from Minneapolis in the north to Memphis in the south was badly affected by the flood.

Why?
- The Mississippi drains water from over 30 per cent of the USA.
- There had been continuous rainfall from April to July saturating soils and leading to rapid overland flow.
- Heavy thunderstorms in June throughout the Midwest delivered record rainfall.
- The Mississippi is fed by over 100 major tributaries. The Missouri and Tennessee rivers carried vast quantities of water into the Mississippi which caused flooding around the **confluences** (where rivers joined).

What happened?
- The river rose to record levels causing **levées** to collapse.
- 8000 homes were destroyed and 37,000 people were evacuated.
- 47 people were killed.
- Des Moines and St Louis were left without water and power supplies.
- One million acres of soya bean and corn crops were ruined.
- Roads, railways and bridges were cut off
- Sewage contaminated water supplies.
- **Sedimentation** blocked navigable channels and disrupted shipping.

Test Yourself — Themes
Sort the factors opposite under the headings, 'natural' and 'human'.

Hints and Tips!
Don't forget, people can often make floods worse as well as prevent them.

Hints and Tips!
Try and fit the factors that make floods more likely into your case studies.

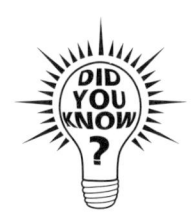

Did You Know?
80 per cent of Bangladesh is a floodplain of the Ganges and Brahmaputra rivers.

Floods

How can people prevent flooding?

Know your case study

Tennessee Valley, USA

Following the earlier floods of 1927 and 1973 a massive flood prevention scheme was introduced by the Tennessee Valley Authority (TVA). The main points of the scheme included:
- over 300 dams were built to create reservoirs to store excess water safely
- existing earth levées were reinforced with concrete
- meanders were removed and the channel straightened to speed up the flow
- dredging of the river increased the channel capacity
- an extra channel or spillway was constructed to divert floodwater to specially built reservoirs
- afforestation of the upland slopes was undertaken to intercept rainfall and reduce run-off and soil erosion.

However, despite these efforts the 1993 flood could not be prevented. This serves as a reminder that natural processes are often out of our control.

Know your case study

Bangladesh

Despite the scale of the Mississippi flood loss of life was kept to a minimum. Floods usually bring far greater loss of life in LEDCs such as Bangladesh. Why is this?
- The economy of Bangladesh is dominated by primary exports. The most productive land is often found on the floodplains due to a gradual build up of rich alluvium deposited by the floodwater. The fertile land becomes densely populated.
- The country's GNP is very low and the government cannot afford to invest in expensive flood defences.
- Floods recur frequently. Many people have not recovered from one flood when the next one occurs.
- Many people live at subsistence level (they grow only just enough food to feed themselves). A flood can destroy food supplies, kill livestock and result in widespread starvation.
- Medical and emergency services are less well equipped to cope with the aftermath.
- Many people live in isolated rural settlements and may not receive help for some time.

Country	MEDC	LEDC
Date		
Location		
Causes		
Social effects		
Economic effects		
Solution or prevention		

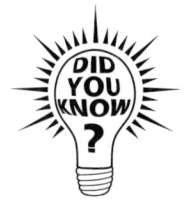

Did you know?

A scheme to prevent flooding in one location often increases the risk of flooding downstream.

Test Yourself

Places

1. Which of these factors will increase the likelihood of a flood: deep soil, steep slopes, urbanization, permeable rock, thin soil, high drainage density, prolonged heavy rainfall?

2. Name and locate a flood that you have studied.

3. Give five effects the flood had on this place.

4. List ways people have tried to prevent or control the flood.

5. Using your notes and textbook produce a table, like the one on the left, comparing floods in a named LEDC and MEDC.

Drought

Key words and definitions

drought	A long period without significant amounts of rainfall.
desertification	The process by which land gradually becomes desert.
soil erosion	The removal of soil by wind and rain.
deforestation	Cutting down of forests.
appropriate technology	Cheap, easily maintained technology which does not increase dependence on MEDCs for fuel or parts.
afforestation	Planting of forests.

The severity of a drought depends on many things. Two of the most important are:
- population size - if the demand for water is high and supplies are low a drought will have a bigger impact on people's lives
- the level of the country's development will affect people's ability to cope in times of drought.

Drought in the UK

The UK has experienced a significant rise in the number of droughts, particularly in the south east. However droughts in the UK tend not to cause the hardship we associate with LEDCs. Some of the ways people can cope in times of drought include:
- re-using bath water for watering the garden
- obeying hose pipe bans imposed by water authorities
- not leaving the taps running when brushing teeth
- having a water butt in the garden to collect any rain that does fall.

Effects of drought in the UK
- Falling river levels increase the concentration of pollutants which causes fish and other aquatic life to die.
- The lack of irrigation may lead to lower crop yields.
- As clay soils dry out they contract often causing the foundations of property to become unstable.
- Water may have to be rationed using standpipes.

Hints and Tips!
Different countries have a different definition of drought. For instance what may seem like a drought in the UK will be considered normal in drier regions.

Know your case study

Drought and desertification in LEDCs: Life in the Sahel
The Sahel is a semi-arid region in Africa on the southern edge of the Sahara desert. The region suffers from frequent droughts that have terrible consequences.

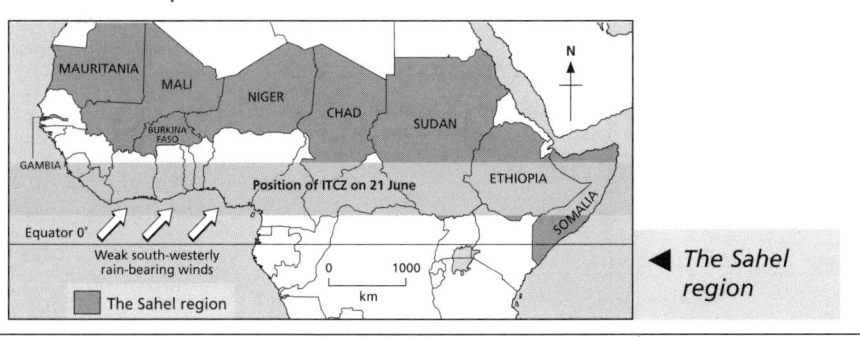

◀ The Sahel region

Hints and Tips!
Droughts occur in many parts of the world. However, deaths as a result of drought are confined to LEDCs where the people are already living on the edge and cannot cope with more hardship.

Drought

Case study continued

Causes of drought in the Sahel
- Droughts occur when the annual rain season fails to arrive. The rains fail because of high pressure over North Africa blocking the northerly migration of the ITCZ (low pressure zone) which brings the rain belts from the south east.
- The impact of drought is worsened by human activities such as collection of firewood and overcultivation and overgrazing which leaves the soils unprotected from the sun.

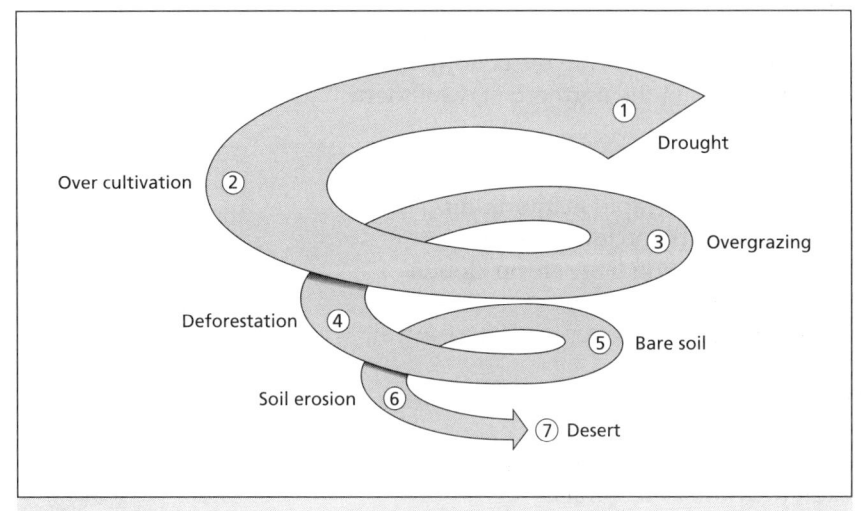

▲ *The downward spiral of desertification*

(1) Drought
(2) Over cultivation
(3) Overgrazing
(4) Deforestation
(5) Bare soil
(6) Soil erosion
(7) Desert

The effects of drought
- Dry soils are easily eroded by the wind and washed away when the rains finally arrive.
- Soil erosion due to drought and mismanagement leads to desertification where land can no longer support vegetation growth and turns to a desert.
- Drought is also a cause of rural to urban migration: when crops fail people are forced to move to the cities in search of food and work.
- In the worst cases droughts can result in terrible famines and the starvation of millions of people and livestock.
- Burkina Faso suffered a prolonged period of drought from 1979-84.

Living with drought and preventing desertification
- Supply short-term food aid to prevent starvation as in the Sudan in 1998.
- Improve water supplies by building dams to store water for use in dry periods.
- Build wells deeper so they will not dry up when the water table falls as in northern Senegal.
- Introduce the use of drought-resistant crops as in Nigeria.
- Building earth traps to prevent soil from being washed away.
- Start **afforestation** schemes which can increase interception and reduce overland flow and so prevent soil erosion. Community-based schemes bring the extra benefits of fodder and fuelwood and income from forest products. Examples of such schemes have been successful in reducing soil erosion in the Sahel and other countries such as Nepal.

Hints and Tips!
For more detail about the case study, refer to your textbook.

Hints and Tips!
The best schemes for the Sahel are small scale, low-cost and use **appropriate technology**.

Test Yourself

Places
1. Name three countries affected by drought in the Sahel.
2. List three effects of drought in a named Sahel region.
3. Give three ways the effects of droughts can be managed.

Tropical storms

Tropical storms occur in areas of extremely low pressure that develop in tropical latitudes. In the Atlantic they are known as tropical storms. In the Pacific they are known as cyclones. You may also have studied typhoons and willy-willies.

What is a tropical storm?
A tropical storm revolves and can produce wind speeds over 200km/h, heavy rainfall and high seas.

Where do tropical storms occur?
Tropical storms develop over tropical seas between 5 and 20 degrees latitude. Here high temperatures and moist air provide the conditions that cause tropical storms. Tropical storms occur in the northern and southern hemispheres.

Why do tropical storms occur?
- High temperatures over tropical seas cause rapid **evaporation**. The warm, moist air rises creating areas of extreme low pressure.
- Warm, moist air cools and condenses creating large storm clouds. **Condensation** leads to high levels of rainfall.
- Warm, moist air is sucked in from the surface to replace the rising air creating strong winds.
- The Coriolis force (spin of the Earth) encourages the storm to rotate producing a characteristic spiral formation.
- An 'eye' forms at the centre of the storm as air sinks back towards the ground creating an area of high pressure as it spirals.

What problems do tropical storms cause?
No two tropical storms are the same but there is a similar pattern of devastation for each.
- The high winds cause widespread structural damage to buildings and blow down power and communication cables.
- The high rainfall can trigger flooding and mudslides that damage roads and bridges and can destroy crops.
- The high seas can result in tidal surges that flood coastal areas leading to loss of life.
- Shipping and air travel must be diverted.

How can tropical storms be predicted and controlled?
Tropical storms can be monitored using satellite systems. The progress of a storm is tracked allowing scientists to forecast the areas most at risk. The US constantly monitors the Atlantic Ocean for signs of tropical storms allowing time to prepare for the storm and limit loss of life. Tropical storm warnings are issued twelve hours prior to the arrival of a storm. In Florida most homes have storm shelters. People without access to a shelter are encouraged to move to the bathroom, which is considered the safest part of a house. Windows are boarded up to prevent injury from breaking glass. People store food and water for the immediate aftermath of the storm. Evacuation of the high-risk areas helps to save lives.

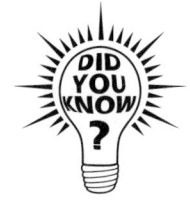

Did You Know?

In the northern hemisphere tropical storms turn anti-clockwise and track northwards. In the southern hemisphere tropical storms turn clockwise and track southwards.

Test Yourself

Themes

1. Explain why storms develop over tropical seas.
2. Name and locate a tropical storm you have studied.
3. Give two social and two economic effects of a tropical storm you have studied.
4. List four ways people can prepare for or control the effects of a tropical storm.

Tropical storms

Know your case study

Hurricane Georges

When?
- Hurricane Georges tore through the Caribbean in September 1998.

Where?
- The Caribbean islands took the brunt of the hurricane's strength with the Dominican Republic being worst hit.
- Other islands affected included Haiti and St Kitts.
- The hurricane then blew over the Florida Keys in the USA.

Effects in the Dominican Republic
- Over 100,000 people were made homeless.
- The death toll was estimated to be over 1000.
- The eastern side of the island was devastated.
- 80 per cent of roads and bridges were damaged.
- 90 per cent of the plantations were destroyed.
- Disease spread due to lack of clean water and sanitation.
- The economic cost to the island was estimated to be $2 billion.

Effects in Florida
- Power supplies to 200,000 homes in Miami and all homes in the Florida Keys were cut off, but services were restored quickly.
- Communications were down and the over-sea highway connecting the Keys to mainland Florida was cut off due to a 3m storm surge.
- Airports at Miami and Fort Lauderdale were temporarily closed.
- The Federal Emergency Management Agency offered $74 million in aid. No such agency exists in the Dominican Republic.
- Trees were uprooted and roofs were damaged.
- No fatalities were reported due to a mandatory evacuation order.

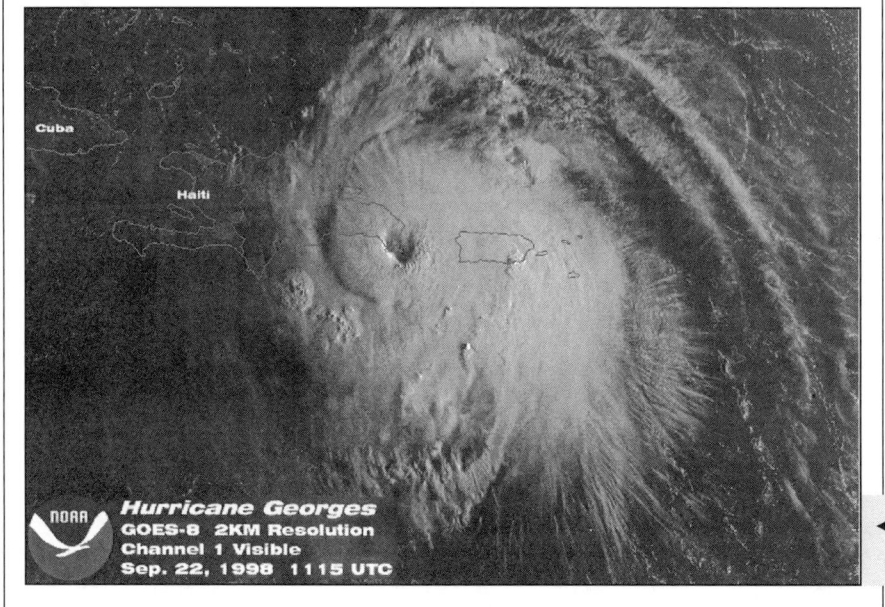

◀ Satellite image of Hurricane Georges

The economic and social effects were much greater in the Caribbean islands than in the Florida Keys. US AID and the Red Cross and many other organizations gave help in the form of emergency food and water supplies, medicines and shelter. Long-term economic support is needed to help with the reconstruction of the Caribbean island's economy.

Hints and Tips!

The damage in the USA is confined to coastal regions because a hurricane loses power as it blows onto land. The loss of power occurs because:

- evaporation is reduced
- temperatures fall as the hurricane tracks polewards
- friction reduces the wind speeds.

Natural hazards and people

Exam practice – higher level paper

B5 This question is about Natural Hazards and People.

(a) Study the figure below.

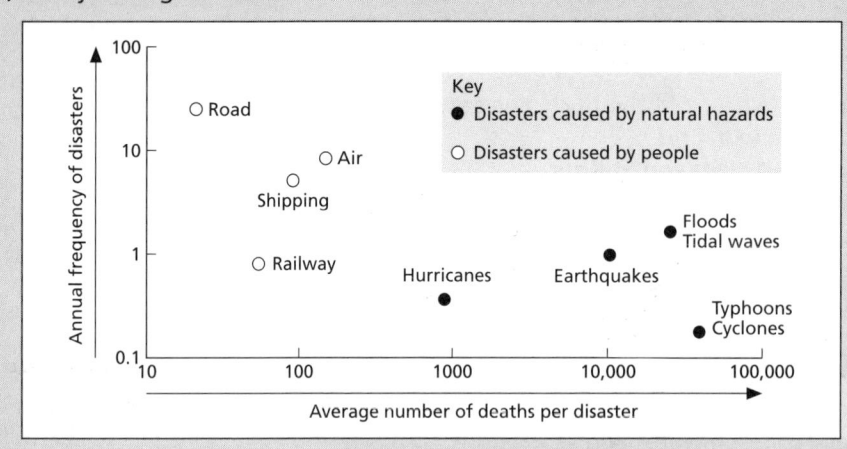

◀ *Disaster frequency*

What is:
(i) the annual frequency of major railway disasters?
(ii) the average number of deaths from major earthquakes? [2]

(b) Compare the frequency and number of deaths for transport accidents and natural disasters. [2]

Study the information about flooding in the Mississippi Basin in 1927 and 1993.

Flood statistics

Date	1927	1993
Time of year	April/May	June/July
Rainfall	Normal	4 × normal
Area affected	Lower valley	Upper valley
Area flooded (sq km)	67,000	81,000
People evacuated	60,000	74,000
Deaths	100s	47
Damage ($ million)	4,400	11,000

▼ *The Mississippi river basin, USA*

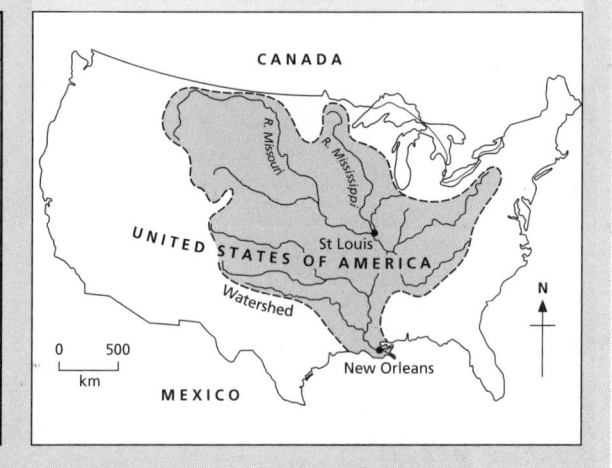

(c) Which flood, in your opinion, was the greater disaster? Give reasons for your answer. [4]

(d) Engineers have constructed many costly schemes to control rivers like the Mississippi. What benefits or problems have these schemes brought to people living on floodplains? [4]

(e) (i) Name and describe the location of a natural hazard, which you have studied, other than flooding.
(ii) Explain the causes of the hazard.
(iii) Describe how the hazard has been or could be predicted and its effects controlled. [8]

[Total 20 marks]

Summary

Natural hazards and people

Theme 2 check list

	Confident	Not bad	Needs more work
The nature and distribution of natural hazards			
I know the different types of natural hazard	✓	☐	☐
I know where the following occur:			
volcanoes and earthquakes	✓	☐	☐
tropical storms	✓	☐	☐
floods	✓	☐	☐
drought	✓	☐	☐
What causes natural hazards?			
I know what causes:			
volcanic eruptions and earthquakes	✓	☐	☐
tropical storms	☐	☐	☐
floods	✓	☐	☐
drought	✓	☐	☐
I know how people's activities, such as overgrazing, deforestation and the growth of towns and cities can have an impact on natural hazards	✓	☐	☐
The effects of natural hazards on people			
I know what the different effects of natural hazards are:			
in rural and urban areas	✓	☐	☐
in densely and sparsely populated areas	✓	☐	☐
in MEDCs and LEDCs	✓	☐	☐
I know how people can be protected from natural hazards	✓	☐	☐
I know how some natural hazards can be predicted	✓	☐	☐
I know how some natural hazards can be controlled	✓	☐	☐

Test Yourself

Tick the boxes – if you still do not understand seek help from your teacher.

Hints and Tips!

Write down the names of your chosen case studies. Ask your teacher to check your choices.

Know your case studies

Which real places have you studied as an example of:
- Local microclimate   name and location _____
- volcanoes – causes, effects, responses   name and location _____
- earthquakes– causes, effects, responses   name and location _____
- tropical storms – causes, effects, responses   name and location _____
- floods – causes, effects, responses   name and location _____
- droughts – causes, effects, responses   name and location _____
- tsunamis   name and location _____
- bush fire   name and location _____
- fog   name and location _____

Theme 3: Economic systems and development

For this theme you will need to know about:
- economic systems
- the location of different economic activities
- economic activity, growth and change
- international disparities, trade and interdependence.

The economy is an organized system of activities in communities which generate wealth. It is usually subdivided into four industrial sectors:
- **Primary sector** activities generate wealth through the collection or exploitation of natural resources. Industries in this sector include agriculture, mining, forestry and fishing.
- **Secondary sector** activities generate wealth through the processing of natural resources and the manufacturing of goods from raw materials. Industries in this sector include steel making, ship building, textiles, food processing and many others.
- **Tertiary sector** activities generate wealth through the provision of services. Activities in this sector include personal services such as retail, tourism, education and health care and professional services such as accountancy and banking.
- **Quaternary sector** activities are often called information services and generate wealth through the use of information and new technologies. Activities include high-tech industries and research and development.

Hints and Tips!
It will be useful to learn the definitions of these economic sectors and an example of the types of activities they include.

Key words and definitions

economic structure	The proportion of a workforce employed in each sector of the economy.
economic system	The inputs, processes and outputs of an economic activity.
Gross Domestic Product (GDP)	The total wealth created by a country's economic activities not including income from foreign investment per year, usually measured per person.
Gross National Product (GNP)	The total wealth created by a country's economic activities including income from foreign investment.

Key Ideas
- All countries have an economy which generates the GDP. The amount of GDP generated by each sector (primary, secondary, tertiary) of the economy can be used as a measure of development for each country.
- Industries are systems made up of inputs, processes and outputs.
- The location of industry is dependent on human and physical factors.
- Economic activities change over time.

Using examples from at least two sectors of the economy you must learn about economic systems, the factors affecting an industry's location, and recent changes in the industry. A systems approach to the study of industries simply breaks down the overall activity into three sections – inputs, processes and outputs. This makes it easier to compare different industries. Inputs are the things needed before production can begin. The processes are the jobs that need to be done in the making or development of the product. Outputs are the final products and waste products created.

Primary industry: farming

Key words and definitions

arable	The cultivation of crops.
pastoral	The rearing of livestock.
mixed	Growing crops and rearing livestock.
subsistence	Farmers grow enough only to feed themselves.
commercial	Products are sold for profit.
intensive	Agriculture that requires a lot of inputs, such as labour.
extensive	Agriculture that uses few inputs.

Agricultural systems

There are many different types of agriculture around the world. Each type of farm has a different economic system – the inputs, processes and outputs will vary in type and quantity.

Traditionally, the type of farming in a region depended on factors such as the climate, relief, soil type, population size, and access to market. Many of these limiting factors can be overcome using modern technology.

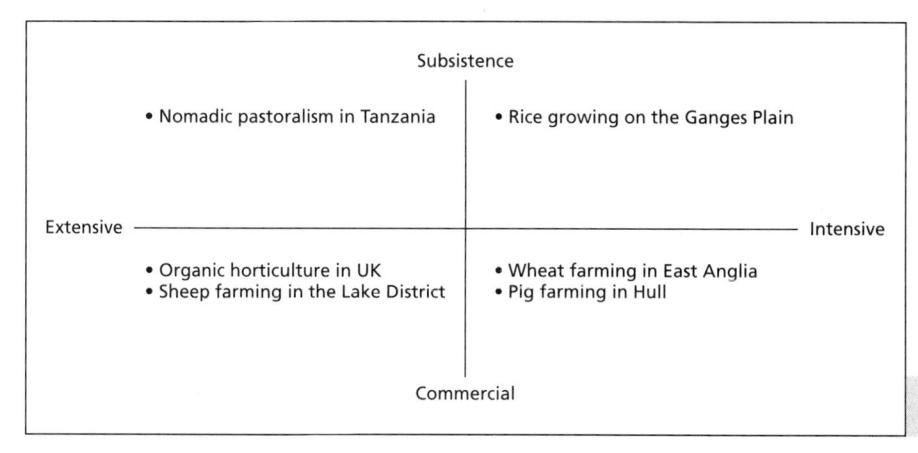

```
                        Subsistence
                            |
  • Nomadic pastoralism     |  • Rice growing on the Ganges Plain
    in Tanzania             |
                            |
  Extensive ────────────────┼──────────────── Intensive
                            |
  • Organic horticulture    |  • Wheat farming in East Anglia
    in UK                   |  • Pig farming in Hull
  • Sheep farming in the    |
    Lake District           |
                            |
                        Commercial
```

◀ *The agriculture matrix*

Climate The hours of sunshine, amount of rainfall and seasonal temperatures will affect the growing season. Cooler, wet climates are not suitable for arable farming but produce lush pasture for pastoral farming. Irrigation can overcome the problem of low rainfall. Cool temperatures can be overcome by cultivating crops in greenhouses.

Relief and altitude Steep slopes are unsuitable for machinery and tend to have thin soils and are unsuitable for arable farming. Upland areas tend to have higher rainfall and are more suited to pastoral farming.

Soil type Deep, fertile, well-drained soils are needed for arable farming. Pasture and rough grazing can grow on less fertile soils. Artificial fertilizers can be added to improve yields. In areas with acid soils lime can be added. Waterlogged soils can be drained.

Access to market Farms that produce perishable goods such as milk and eggs must be close to urban areas. Farms producing non-perishable goods such as livestock can locate in more remote areas. Improvements in transport such as refrigeration mean farms do not need to be close to their markets.

Hints and Tips!

Not all farms are the same. You may be asked to describe a farm you have studied so make sure you learn specific facts about that farm's location, inputs, outputs and processes rather than giving a general description of a typical farm. When revising a case study you must know about the system involved, the reason for its location, recent changes and the social, economic and physical impacts the changes have had. The case study provided deals with each of these points. It is a good idea to view your own notes in the same way.

Economic systems and development

Commercial agriculture in the UK

Most farms in the UK can be described as open systems. This means that the outputs are sold leaving the system and only some of the profits are reinvested in the system.

The UK has many different types of agriculture but most are classed as commercial in that the produce is sold to a market rather than grown for the farmer's own use.

> *Hints and Tips!*
> Learning summary diagrams of the economic systems can save you a lot of time in the exam!

Know your case study

Vine House Farm, a commercial grain farm in the UK

Location The farm is situated in East Anglia between Peterborough and Spalding.

Reason for its location The flat land and well drained soil provides an ideal location. The region has a long growing season, the climate being warm, dry and sunny providing ideal growing conditions.

The Fens of East Anglia
Table of temperatures, rainfall and sunshine hours

	J	F	M	A	M	J	J	A	S	O	N	D
Temperature (°C)	3	4	6	8	12	15	17	16	13	10	7	4
Rainfall (mm)	45	30	30	45	45	36	60	45	50	45	40	35
Sunshine hours	1.6	2.3	3.8	4.8	6.1	6.8	6.1	5.8	4.6	3.3	1.9	1.3

Size The farm now covers 758ha.

Ownership The farm is privately owned by the Watts family.

Recent changes The farm has specialised and intensified in order to become more productive.
- less labour
- larger fields
- more machinery
- no livestock
- more inorganic chemicals
- removal of hedgerows and drainage

System diagram for Vine House Farm

Inputs	Processes	Outputs
• Weather	• Maintenance	• Oilseed rape
• 758ha land	• Drilling and sowing	• Linseed
• 8 workers and casual labour in harvest time	• Spraying	• Wheat
• Tractors	• Weeding	• Sugar beet
• Combine harvester	• Harvesting	• Peas
• Seed	• Ploughing	

Test Yourself

Places

Draw a system diagram for a farm you have studied. Use the headings 'inputs', 'processes' and 'outputs'.

Economic activity, growth and change

Key Ideas
- Economic activity has undergone significant change in the post-war period. These changes have been due to developments in technology and transport and to changing government policy.
- Why do some places grow while others decline?
- What are the effects of economic change in the quality of life in different places?

Key words and definitions

the CAP	The Common Agricultural Policy was set up by the EU to try and increase productivity, control prices and improve farm incomes.
intensification	The process of increasing outputs from existing land.
surplus	Produce which is not needed by the existing market.
diversification	Varying the use of farmland to reduce surplus production.
agribusiness	Large-scale industrial style farms.
eutrophication	An increase in the level of nutrients which leads to more rapid plant growth.

Following the Second World War the British Government tried to make Britain self-sufficient in food production and provide the country with a reliable supply of food at reasonable prices. Thus began the drive towards **intensification** of agriculture. When Britain joined the EU in 1973 (EEC as it was then) it came under the Common Agricultural Policy which used a system of subsidies and guaranteed prices to protect farms from competition from cheap imports and encourage farmers to increase production.

The effects of the CAP
The subsidies and guaranteed prices were an incentive to farmers to increase agricultural production. This was mainly done by intensifying use of existing land. Farmers used several methods to increase yields:
- drainage of wet meadows
- irrigation
- the use of specialized machinery
- the increased use of chemical fertilizers
- the use of herbicides, pesticides and fungicides to reduce crop wastage
- specialization in one or two crops.

Consequences of intensification
- Larger farms benefited more than small family farms resulting in a trend towards larger farms as smaller farms were amalgamated by large-scale **agribusiness**.
- The incomes of farmers increased.
- The use of machinery led to the removal of hedgerows to increase the size of fields. This destroyed wildlife habitats and resulted in increased soil erosion.
- The use of chemical fertilizers resulted in the **eutrophication** (nutrient enrichment) of waterways, such as the Norfolk Broads.
- The use of pesticides and herbicides unbalanced ecosystems.
- Larger fields, with fewer barns and new visually intrusive crops such as oil seed rape and lavender have replaced the traditional 'patchwork' landscape.

Hints and Tips!
You can remember four farming methods of intensifation using the word 'DISC' for **D**rainage, **I**rrigation, **S**pecialization and **C**hemicals.

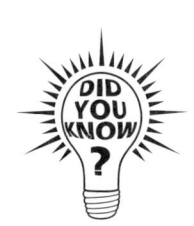

DID YOU KNOW?
The number of tractors on British farms quadrupled between 1950 and 1990!

- The production of wheat, beef, milk and other subsidized products exceeded demand resulting in large surpluses. The surpluses must be stored by the EU which is expensive and absorbs large amounts of the EU budget.
- The intensification of livestock farming has led to concerns about animal rights and the transmission of diseases.

Reforming the CAP

The EU has reformed the CAP in an attempt to reduce surplus production and protect the environment. Policies include:

1 **Set aside** Farmers paid to remove 15 per cent of their land from agricultural production for five years. It was hoped that this would reduce production by 15 per cent but in reality farmers set aside 15 per cent and intensified production on the remaining 85 per cent.
2 **Quotas** The EU introduced quotas. Each farm was given a production quota. Below this the guaranteed price was paid, but if a farm exceeded its quota a levy was charged. This system hit farmers hard and many dairy farmers were forced to sell off part of their herd.
3 **ESAs** The EU designated Environmentally Sensitive Areas. In these areas farmers are paid to use less intensive methods of cultivation thus compensating them for lower yields.
4 **Farm diversification** Farmers are also encouraged to use land for alternative purposes. Many farmers are planting woodland or opening fish farms, building holiday homes and golf courses. Farmers may open up their land as a war games venue for leisure and corporate team-building exercises.

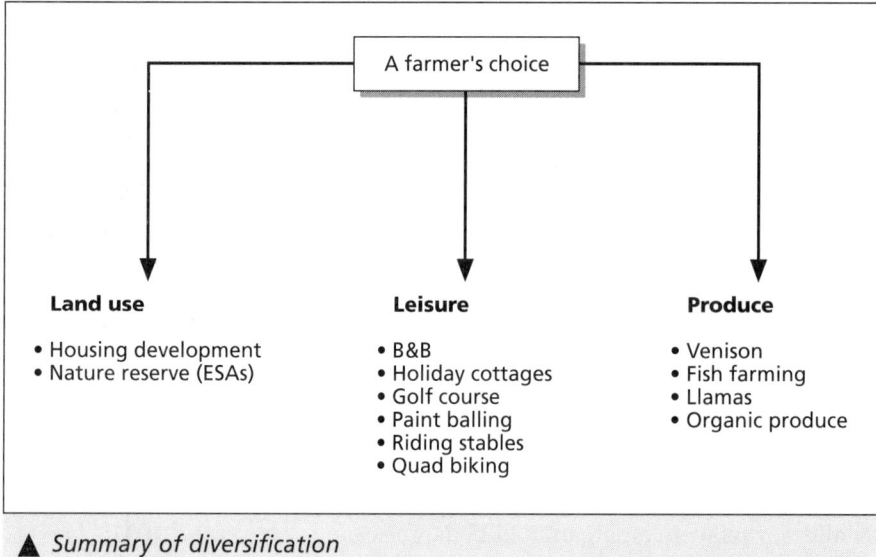

A farmer's choice

Land use
- Housing development
- Nature reserve (ESAs)

Leisure
- B&B
- Holiday cottages
- Golf course
- Paint balling
- Riding stables
- Quad biking

Produce
- Venison
- Fish farming
- Llamas
- Organic produce

▲ *Summary of diversification*

Test Yourself

Places

In your notebook write the heading 'Agriculture in the EU' and answer the following questions.

1 Describe four methods used to increase agricultural production in your chosen region.
2 Give four problems that have resulted from the intensification of agriculture in your chosen region.
3 Describe two measures the EU has introduced to reduce surplus production.
4 For a farm or farms that you have studied describe and explain recent changes to the system.

Agriculture outside the EU

Agriculture in MEDCs outside the EU has also experienced changes as a result of government policy.

Know your case study

Japanese agriculture

Following the Second World War Japan suffered from crippling food shortages. To deal with this the government:

- passed land reforms which abolished the tenant farm system which was dominated by large land owners.
- created small holdings which would give each household a basic living.
- imposed strict trade barriers to protect Japanese farms from cheap rice imports from the Philippines and Thailand.
- offered Japanese farmers a guaranteed price for their rice which at times was six times that given on the world market!

This protection helped to support an inefficient agricultural system dominated by small family-owned farms.

Changing times

- Even with subsidies, incomes in rural Japan have not kept pace with those in urban areas. Rural areas, such as Hokkaido and the Ishikara Plain, have experienced out-migration where the young move to the cities leaving behind the elderly and creating a shortage of labour in agricultural areas.
- As Japanese society became influenced by the West the market for rice has decreased in favour of wheat, vegetables and dairy produce. Farmers were encouraged to reduce their production of rice and grow alternative crops by the government who lifted trade barriers and reduced subsidies on rice.
- New hardy strains of rice have been developed which can grow in the cooler climates of Hokkaido and Honshu. This region around the Ishikara Plain is now the major rice-growing area while land in the south has been opened up for cultivation of new crops such as wheat and soft fruit.
- In areas such as Aichi, Shizuoka and Okayama, closer to the urban markets, rice has been replaced by vegetables, soft fruit and dairy farming. Farms use technology such as hydroponics to cultivate crops under glass allowing fruit and vegetables to be grown in the cooler plateau regions as well as the warmer areas in the southern islands of Kyushu and Shikoku.

Test Yourself

Places

1. List three changes that have affected Japanese agriculture.
2. Describe how and why the distribution of agriculture has changed in Honshu, Japan, or in another MEDC you have studied.

Economic development in rural India

Key Ideas
- Agricultural improvement has been used as a method of economic development in many LEDCs.
- Changes to agricultural systems can have far-reaching social and economic and environmental impacts.

Economic systems and development

Key words and definitions

higher yielding varieties (HYVs) Varieties of crops which are genetically modified to produce higher yields.

Green Revolution The use of HYVs and other technology to increase agricultural productivity in LEDCs.

Agricultural production in India was facing crisis in the 1960s. Famines were worsening; the import of grain was causing financial difficulties for the Indian government. Both 1966 and 1967 saw falling harvests. The agricultural sector was near ruin.

HYVs, such as IR8 (miracle rice), were introduced to India in the late 1960s in an attempt to increase rice production and move away from subsistence farming. The higher yielding varieties were not as hardy as traditional varieties and needed irrigation and fertilizers, which in turn meant an increase in the use of machinery. These developments brought with them great social, economic and environmental consequences.

Know your case study

India and the Green Revolution

Location The Punjab in the north west on the Indo-Gangetic Plain.

Benefits of the Green Revolution
- The production of rice doubled in some areas of the Punjab.
- Farm incomes rose.
- India was no longer dependent on food aid.
- Provided the stable agricultural sector needed for industrial development.

Social problems created by the Green Revolution
- Rich farmers with more than 4ha of land could afford the irrigation systems and fertilizers required for the HYVs and they benefited from increased productivity. The poorer farmers with small farms could not afford the technology and had to take out loans which they could not afford.
- The mechanization of agriculture led to the eviction of tenant farmers and fuelled rural to urban migration.
- The technological changes brought an increase in non-traditional crops such as wheat at the expense of staple food crops such as maize and millet. This meant that the poorer people had to spend more money on food.
- Women traditionally tended the rice paddies. As machinery was introduced, the role of women was reduced.

Economic problems
- The gap between the rich and poor widened.
- The need to import fuel, machinery and fertilizers increased the trade deficit.

Environmental problems
- Irrigation led to salinization (increase in salts and minerals) of the soil.
- Machinery compacted the soil reducing infiltration thereby increasing dependence on irrigation.
- Soil lost structure as no organic matter was ploughed back into the ground.
- Agricultural chemicals contaminated ground water supplies which affected the rural supplies of drinking water from wells.

Test Yourself

Places

1. How was productivity increased by the Green Revolutuion?

2. Give two benefits of the Green Revolution.

3. Give a social, an economic and an environmental problem created by the Green Revolution in the Punjab.

4. Using your own study notes list the advantages and disadvantages of a named agricultural development in an LEDC.

Secondary industry

Key Ideas
- The location of traditional manufacturing secondary industries was decided according to access to raw materials, power, labour, transport and a market.
- Secondary industries change location in response to changes in transport, technology and government policy.
- Modern industries are 'footloose' and do not depend on any particular factor of industrial location.
- Secondary industries grow and decline over time.

Key words and definitions

break-of-bulk site A point where goods are unloaded, ready for distribution, and transport costs are increased.

bulk-reducing industry An industry where the mass of the raw materials is greater than the mass of the finished product.

bulk-increasing industry An industry where the mass of the product is greater than the mass of the raw materials.

footloose industry Light or high-tech industries which have considerable freedom of location.

industrial inertia A process which keeps industry and people in a place long after the reason for the location has gone.

multiplier effect A knock-on effect leading to economic growth as a result of new investment.

The location of traditional industry

When deciding where to locate a traditional manufacturing industry access to inputs such as land, power, raw materials, labour, transport, market and capital were taken into account. Most traditional industries such as steel and textiles developed in the nineteenth century and depended on coal power and heavy raw materials. As coal is bulky and was expensive to transport most factories were built on the coalfields of South Wales, the Midlands and Yorkshire. Most traditional industries were **bulk reducing**. It was more expensive to transport the bulky raw materials than it was to transport the finished product. Factories were tied to locations close to raw materials. The employment attracted people to the coalfields and gradually the industrial urban areas developed. Although much of this industry has declined the remaining plants tend to stay in the same area because it is too costly to relocate. This is known as **industrial inertia**.

The location of modern industry

Most modern industries are '**footloose**'. This means that they are not tied to only one location factor, unlike the traditional heavy industries (such as iron and steel). These footloose industries include electronics, light manufacturing and high-tech industries. However, these new types of industries have location factors of their own:

- **accessibility** – favourable sites are close to motorway junctions and airports for the distribution of goods and the transportation of components and raw materials.
- **workforce** – firms need to be close to a supply of skilled labour.
- **environment** – footloose industries prefer a good quality environment. For this reason they opt for greenfield sites away from the pollution and congestion of traditional industrial areas.
- **amenities** – a highly skilled workforce tends to be mobile. Workers are attracted by good quality housing, leisure facilities and schools.

Economic systems and development

Key changes in the location can be summarized as:
- an urban to rural shift
- a north to south shift.

These changes in industrial location have had a dramatic impact on the traditional industrial regions and the new up and coming regions.

Hints and Tips!

Theme 4 describes the effect of industrial relocation on the inner cities.

Know your case study

South Wales, a region in transition

Phase 1: 1800-1900 Industrial growth
The South Wales region experienced rapid industrial growth in the nineteenth century due to the discovery of coal in the valleys.
- Mining towns grew as people flocked to the coalfield in search of work in the pits.
- In 1860 the discovery of limestone and iron ore in the valleys led to the opening of iron and steelworks such as Ebbw Vale.
- Most of the steel produced was exported overseas to British colonies such as India.
- The export of steel resulted in the growth of ports on the south coast such as Swansea and Port Talbot.
- The coal and steel industry provided thousands of jobs in the region.

Phase 2: 1900-1960 Industrial expansion
The steel industry attracted other manufacturing industries to the region in order to cut transport costs. New industries included heavy engineering and car manufacture. These factories turned South Wales into one of Britain's major industrial regions.

Phase 3: 1960-1980 Decline and relocation of traditional industries
- New technology could not be used in the narrow coal seams of the Welsh valleys.
- Pits elsewhere could produce more coal at lower prices and Welsh coal mines became less economical to run.
- Local supplies of limestone and iron ore were exhausted, and what was remaining was poor quality and difficult to extract. Raw materials had to be imported making the production of steel more expensive.
- The 1970s and 1980s brought a world recession which resulted in a falling demand for steel. Many overseas producers of steel were more competitive and Britain began importing steel from the Newly Industrializing Countries (NICs) such as Brazil and South Korea.
- The lack of raw materials, declining market and overseas competition led to the closure of many mines and steelworks in the valleys including Ebbw Vale and the Maerdy Pit which was the last remaining pit in the Rhondda Valley.
- The remaining steelworks depended on the import of raw materials (coal, iron ore and limestone). Eight tonnes of raw material are needed to produce one tonne of steel. Bulky raw materials are expensive to unload and transport so it makes sense to locate at the ports to reduce transport costs. This led to the construction of integrated steelworks on break-of-bulk sites near the ports. These integrated steelworks carry out every stage of the production under one roof and need large areas of flat land and good communications. Llanwern at Newport is an integrated steelworks that currently employs over 3000 workers.

Test Yourself

Themes

1. Study the OS map on page 108. Give three reasons for the location of the Llanwern steelworks (grid reference 36 86 to 39 86).

2. Suggest two reasons why high-tech companies may consider moving to the area.

Case study continued

Phase 4: 1990-2000 Economic regeneration

The closure of mines and steelworks in South Wales had negative social and economic impacts sending out ripples into the local economy. The high unemployment meant there was less money spent in the local area, small businesses and shops closed down, and people moved away in search of work. The decline in population caused local services to decline, schools closed, and the area became depressed. High unemployment led to stress, boredom and related problems such as alcoholism, divorce and crime.

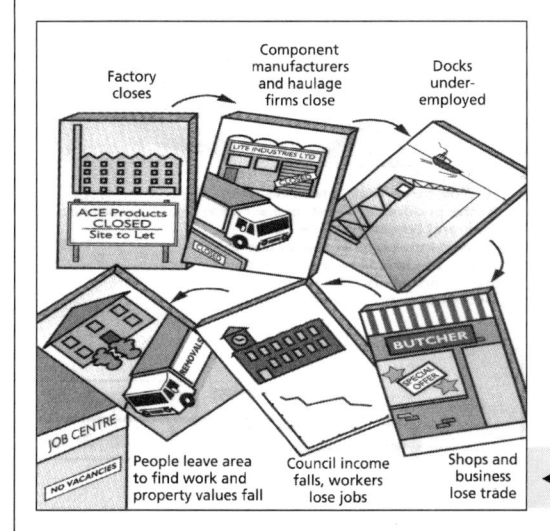

◀ *The knock-on effect*

The government has tried to improve the situation:
- Government began to attract new industries to the region in order to regenerate the local economy. The Valley region was given **assisted area** status and the coastal plain given intermediate status. This gave firms establishing in the region a number of financial incentives such as grants for building, machinery, and training.
- The WDA (Welsh Development Agency) was set up to help attract new industries to the area by promoting the area's status as an ideal industrial location.
- The European Regional Development Fund has invested in site provision, training and access, including an extension to the M4 motorway.
- Industrial estates e.g. Waterton industrial estate, Bridgend, have been built offering low rents, good communications and new modern premises at Swansea, Port Talbot, Bridgend, Cardiff, Caerphilly and Newport.
- Transport has been improved by the construction of a new bridge across the River Severn in the 1990s.

The new firms that have located in South Wales are mainly footloose industries such as high-tech electronics, and automotive firms. An abundant and productive workforce, excellent communications and government incentives attract these industries. Well-known firms that have relocated to the area include SONY at Bridgend and Pencoed, Aiwa hifi and CD factory at Newport and the Hitachi TV and VCR factory at Aberdare. The government hopes that the new firms will create employment and produce a **multiplier effect** in the local economy.

Hints and Tips!

You may well be asked to name a factory or business and describe features of the business. Learning specific facts and figures about inputs, processes and outputs will give you the information needed for top marks!

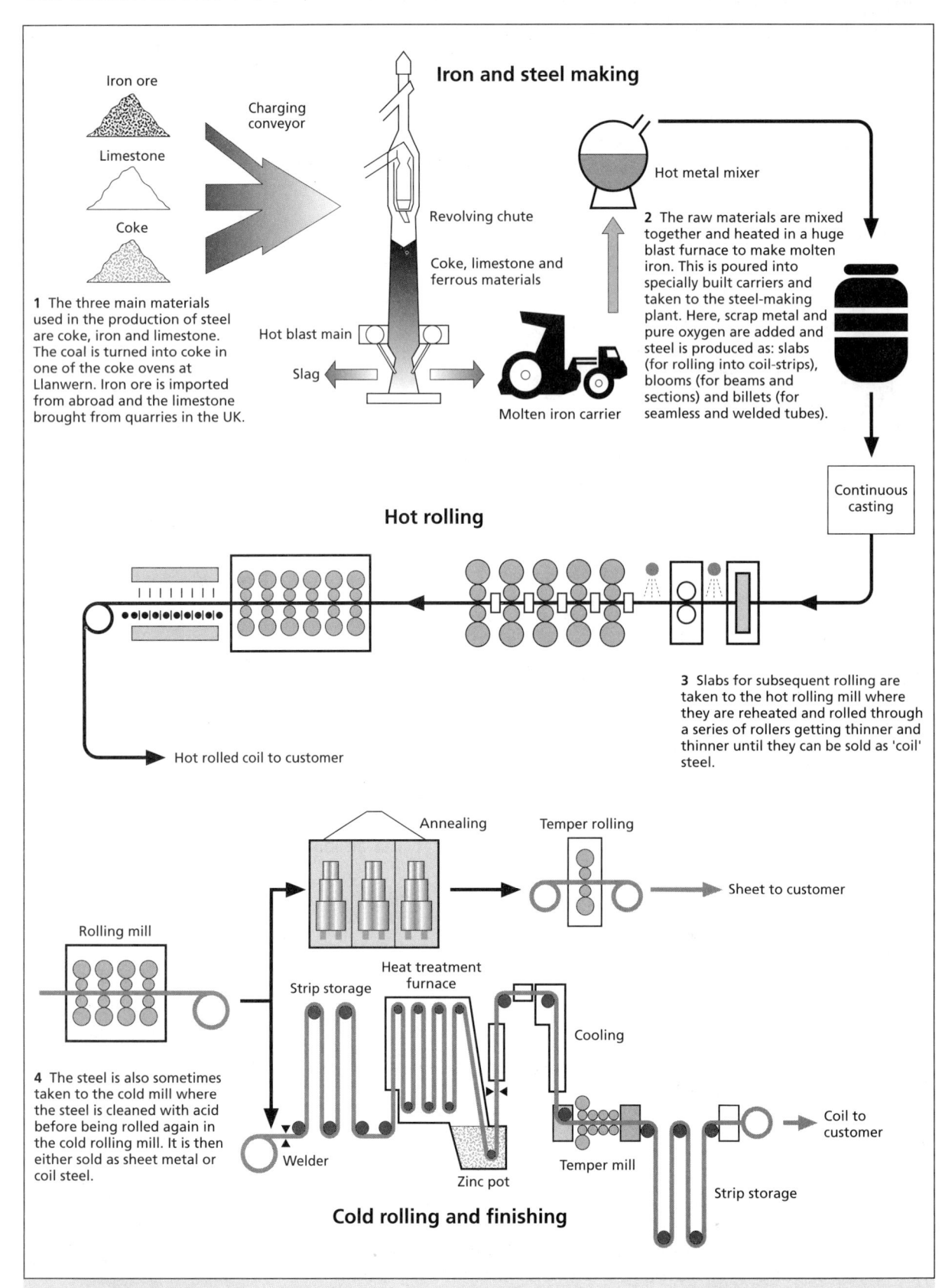

Economic systems and development

The Llanwern steelworks

Iron and steel making

Iron ore
Limestone
Coke

Charging conveyor

Revolving chute

Coke, limestone and ferrous materials

Hot blast main

Slag

Molten iron carrier

Hot metal mixer

1 The three main materials used in the production of steel are coke, iron and limestone. The coal is turned into coke in one of the coke ovens at Llanwern. Iron ore is imported from abroad and the limestone brought from quarries in the UK.

2 The raw materials are mixed together and heated in a huge blast furnace to make molten iron. This is poured into specially built carriers and taken to the steel-making plant. Here, scrap metal and pure oxygen are added and steel is produced as: slabs (for rolling into coil-strips), blooms (for beams and sections) and billets (for seamless and welded tubes).

Continuous casting

Hot rolling

Hot rolled coil to customer

3 Slabs for subsequent rolling are taken to the hot rolling mill where they are reheated and rolled through a series of rollers getting thinner and thinner until they can be sold as 'coil' steel.

Cold rolling and finishing

Rolling mill

Strip storage

Welder

Heat treatment furnace

Zinc pot

Annealing

Temper rolling

Sheet to customer

Cooling

Temper mill

Strip storage

Coil to customer

4 The steel is also sometimes taken to the cold mill where the steel is cleaned with acid before being rolled again in the cold rolling mill. It is then either sold as sheet metal or coil steel.

▲ *The Llanwern steelworks*

Growth and decline of economic activity in a MEDC outside the EU

Key Ideas
- Regions associated with traditional heavy industries are experiencing economic decline.
- Regions associated with high-tech industries are experiencing economic growth.

Key word and definition
deindustrialization   Decline of traditional heavy industries.

Know your case study

Growth and decline in the USA

The Rust Belt
Location
The Rust Belt is a region centred round the Great Lakes in the north east of the USA. It includes the five states of New York, Pennsylvania, Ohio, Michigan and Illinois. The heavy industry of the region has suffered from **deindustrialization**.

Causes of economic decline
The region's economy was centred around steel production using local supplies of iron ore, limestone and coal. The availability of steel attracted heavy industries such as engineering and vehicle manufacturers. They included Ford, General Motors and Chrysler located in Detroit. The steel and motor vehicle industries have suffered a decline for several reasons:
- a world recession has led to a decline in demand for steel
- competition from cheaper, overseas steel producers such as South Korea
- modern alternatives to steel such as plastics
- highly organized workers' trade unions have caused increased labour costs.

Effects of economic decline
It has resulted in:
- high unemployment
- rapid out-migration. There has been a significant decline in population in the last 30 years
- urban decay and dereliction makes it difficult to attract new companies to the region.
- poverty. Out-migration leaves behind those least able to cope.

The Sun Belt
Location
A band of states in the south west including California, Texas, New Mexico, Colorado and Arizona. The region is experiencing economic growth based on high-tech industries.

Economic systems and development

Case study continued

Reasons for growth
Within the Sun Belt, Arizona is one of the most rapidly expanding areas. Companies are attracted to the state by a combination of factors:
- **market** The state capital Phoenix is the seventh largest metropolitan district of the US with a population of 2.4 million. This and the larger markets of West Coast cities (Los Angeles included) are within easy reach by relatively uncongested highways.
- **workforce** The local workforce is skilled and productive. The lack of union activity keeps wages low.
- **access to research** Arizona State University is one of the largest research institutions in the USA.
- **promotion** The region has been widely promoted as an ideal location for companies. The advertisement opposite is for an enterprise zone east of Phoenix. Within enterprise zones like Cobré Valley companies can take advantage of: deed land for development; newly built industrial parks; cheap land; tax savings; relaxed building regulations.
- **agglomeration** High-tech companies attract other companies such as component manufacturers and research companies.

ARIZONA'S
Cobré Valley
(Cobré, pronounced co-bray, is Spanish for copper)

The perfect climate for business.
Strong Economy
Quality, Productive Workforce
Low Cost of Doing Business
Reasonable Regulatory Environment
Attractive Incentives

A traditional quality of life.
Friendly, Small Town Atmosphere
Low Cost of Living
Negligible Crime Rate
Quality Educational System
Efficient, Effective Municipal Services
Outstanding Recreational and Cultural Opportunities
Full Range of Shopping, Dining, and Services
Ideal Year Round Climate

Effects of economic growth
- **employment** Arizona has the third highest rate of employment growth in the USA of 6.2 per cent per year. In Phoenix 56 per cent of manufacturing jobs are with high-tech companies with an average salary of $46,700. Motorola, Teledisic LLC, IBM are all companies which have located in Arizona.
- **population** The region has experienced rapid population growth as people move to the area in search of work. Between 1994 to 1995 Phoenix's population grew by 125,000.
- **urban sprawl** There is a growing housing crisis as construction cannot keep pace with population growth. In Phoenix 50,000 new residential properties are erected every year. As the suburbs spread out into the desert difficulties with water supply grow more serious.
- **immigration** There is a problem of illegal migrants from Mexico crossing the border in search of work. Without the relevant skills for the available jobs, they contribute to the growing number of the population without permanent employment.

Test Yourself

Places
1. For a region in an MEDC you have studied, describe and explain changes in economic activity.
2. How have these changes affected the quality of life in the region?

Regional growth and decline in the EU

Key Ideas
- The EU can be divided into a wealthy, industrialized core and a less developed periphery.
- The EU must try to develop the peripheral regions in order to reduce social and economic variation.
- The EU has important trade links with the rest of the world.

Key words and definitions

core — Regions in which economic activity is concentrated leading to high standards of living.

periphery — Regions that are less developed and have lower standards of living.

infrastructure — Basic communications and service structure of a country

diversification — Broadening of an economic activity, such as a farm offering bed and breakfast.

There are currently fifteen countries in the EU. The level of economic development varies from country to country. The wealthy **core** is often called the 'Hot Banana' as it is a region shaped like a banana stretching from the industrial triangle of northern Italy, across the industrial heartlands of Germany, the Netherlands and northern France, to the south east of the UK. The **periphery** includes less accessible regions such as Ireland, Greece, and Portugal.

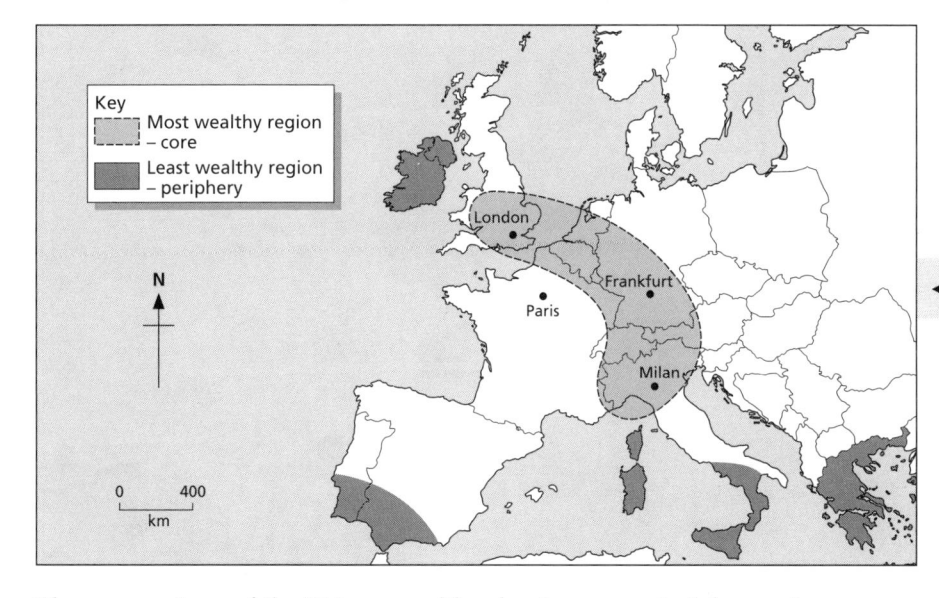

◀ Europe's 'Hot Banana'

The core regions of the EU are wealthy due to raw materials, good communications, well-developed **infrastructure**, accessibility and an urbanized workforce. These factors allow industry to grow and develop, leading to higher incomes and rising standards of living.

The less developed regions of the periphery are remote and inaccessible and lack suitable infrastructure to attract industry. The lack of industry leads to lower incomes and a low standard of living.

The European Regional Development Fund invests money in the less developed regions of Europe to encourage economic growth and improve standards of living.

Places
Cover the map and name three core EU regions and three peripheral regions.

Economic systems and development

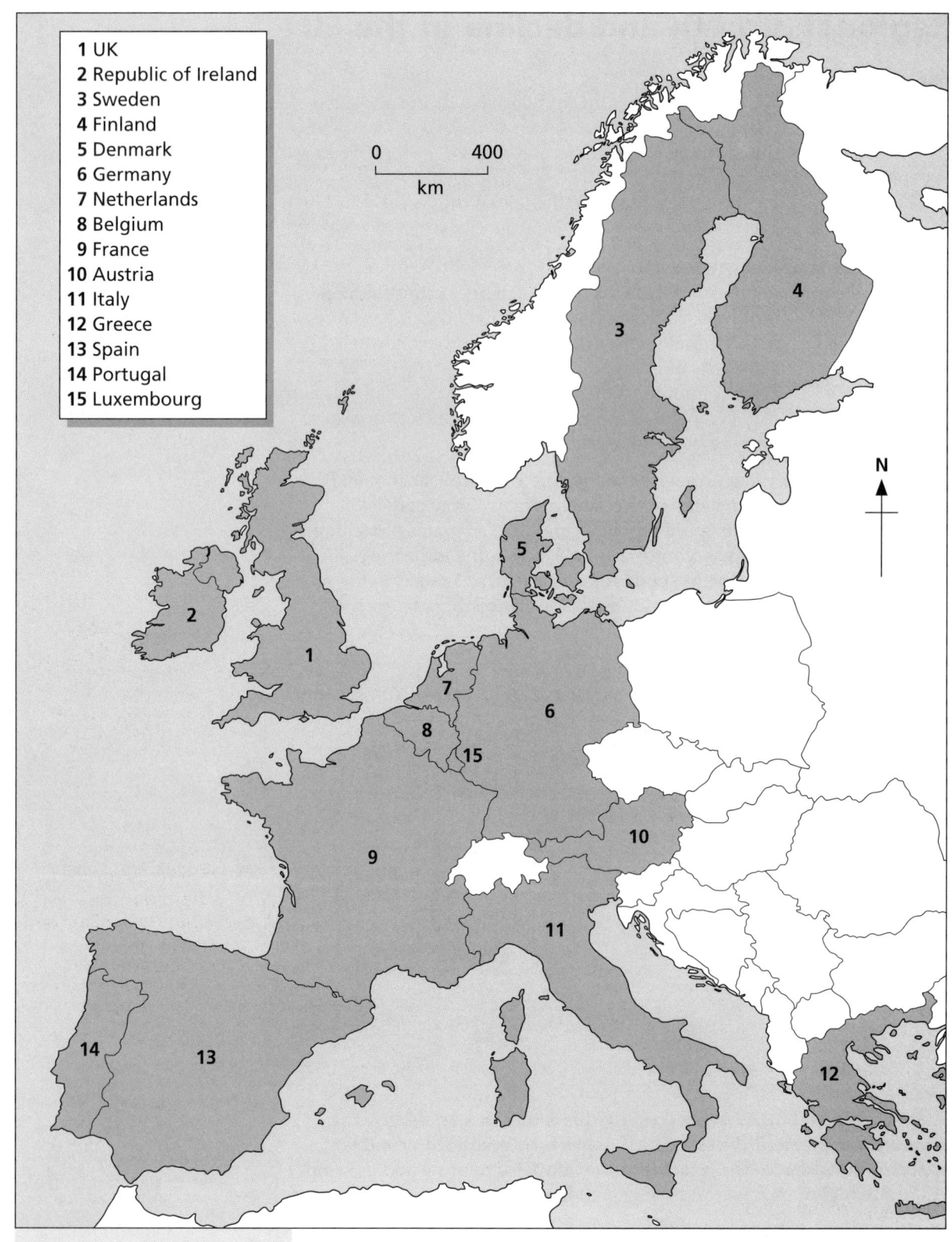

1 UK
2 Republic of Ireland
3 Sweden
4 Finland
5 Denmark
6 Germany
7 Netherlands
8 Belgium
9 France
10 Austria
11 Italy
12 Greece
13 Spain
14 Portugal
15 Luxembourg

▲ *The European Union 1999*

Hints and Tips!

Learn to recognize countries on a map of Europe, as you may well be expected to name them in the exam.

Know your case study

Contrasting EU regions

The North Italian Plain
- The region is flat and communications are well developed.
- The region has good supplies of raw materials, such as iron ore and coal, that attract manufacturing industries such as steel, engineering and textiles.
- The markets of Europe are easily accessible via a system of road and rail tunnels through the alps e.g. Simplon tunnel.
- The cities of Milan, Turin and Genoa provide a large skilled workforce.
- Deep fertile soils and plentiful water supply on the flood plain of the River Po are ideal for agriculture.

Southern Italy: The Mezzogiorno
- The region is dominated by the Apennine Mountains which make communications difficult.
- The lack of accessibility to the markets in the North makes trade difficult.
- The region lacks raw materials and soils are thin and dry.
- Agriculture is the main employer but provides low incomes compared with the industries of the North.
- The region suffers from soil erosion and drought.
- The region is sparsely populated, distributed in small villages perched high up on the barren slopes of the Apennines.

Developing the Mezzogiorno
In 1950 the Italian government established the *Cassa per il Mezzogiorno* – a fund for the development of the southern regions of Italy.
- **Transport and communication** The government paid for a new motorway called the Autostrada del Sol. The new road linked the southern regions with the markets of northern Italy and the rest of Europe.
- **Agricultural reform** Irrigation was improved through large-scale dam building and smaller farm-based schemes. This helped farmers grow more crops. In Apulia large-scale unproductive farms called *latifundia* were broken up and the land was given to individual families. This created 31,000 new farms.
- **Industry** To attract new industries to the Mezzogiorno the government gave financial incentives, such as removing taxes on imported raw materials. This attracted heavy industries that were dependent on imports to the region. In the Naples area a new iron and steel works was established. This attracted other firms such as Alfa Romeo, Olivetti and Pirelli. In Bari, Brindisi and Taranto in the south-east of Italy, a large integrated steelworks developed along with petrochemical firms. In Sicily, Italy's largest car manufacturer, Fiat, established a new assembly plant at Palermo.

Impact of change
While the new industries provided manufacturing jobs and higher wages, they were mainly confined to coastal locations. This increased inequalities between the inland and coastal regions. People continued to leave towns and villages in the interior in search for work in the new industrial developments.

Themes
1. Can you give three reasons why it is difficult to attract industry to the Mezzogiorno?
2. How has the Mezzogiorno's economy changed since 1970?

Places
Produce a table that summarizes the features of another core and peripheral region of the EU. Use the following headings for each region: population; physical features; economy; economic change; factors that make the region different from surrounding areas.

The effects of economic change on the quality of life

Key Ideas
- Tourism is the fastest growing industry in the world.
- Tourism is the world's biggest employer.
- Tourism has been used to develop the economies of many LEDCs.
- Tourism can have both positive and negative impacts on a region.

Key words and definitions
multiplier effect   Direct or indirect consequences of an action, a knock-on effect.
trade deficit   A country is importing more than it is exporting.

Tourism: a blessing or a curse?
The development of air passenger transport and growing competition between airlines has brought the price of air travel tumbling in recent years. These developments have led to an increase in travel to long-haul destinations, bringing many of the world's LEDCs within range of the tourist. Many LEDCs have used tourism to develop their economies. In many ways tourism is an ideal economic activity, however in practice tourism can create problems as well as benefits. The impact on the quality of life in these LEDCs has proved to be far-reaching.

Places
Use your notes to list the advantages and disadvantages tourism has brought to an LEDC you have studied, e.g. Egypt, Barbados, Tanzania.

What does tourism have to offer?
- Many LEDCs have the 'raw materials' for tourism which can include sun, beautiful coastlines, and exotic cultures.
- Most tourists originate in MEDCs and so bring with them the 'tourist dollar' which can provide valuable hard currency.
- Tourism reduces dependence on primary products and increases GDP.
- Tourism can provide employment that can generate a **multiplier effect**.

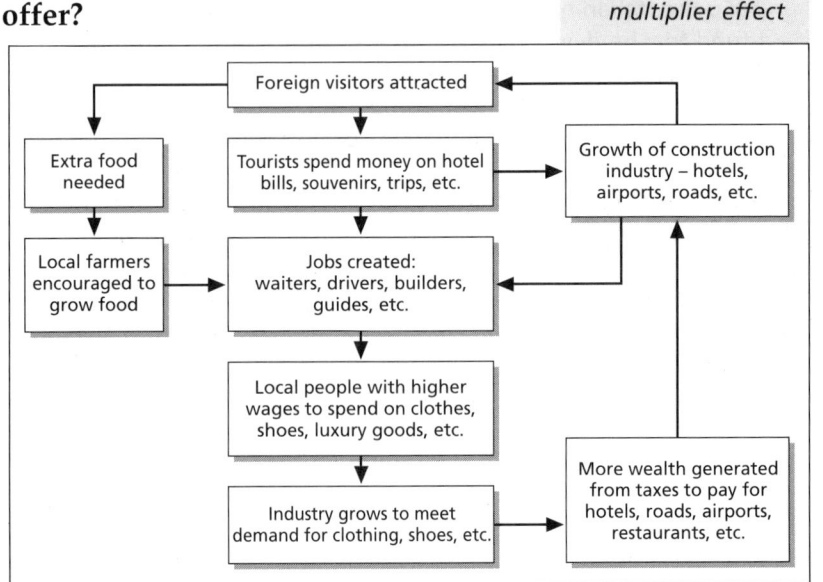

▼ *Tourism and the multiplier effect*

```
Foreign visitors attracted
    ↓
Tourists spend money on hotel bills, souvenirs, trips, etc.
    → Extra food needed → Local farmers encouraged to grow food
    → Growth of construction industry – hotels, airports, roads, etc.
    ↓
Jobs created: waiters, drivers, builders, guides, etc.
    ↓
Local people with higher wages to spend on clothes, shoes, luxury goods, etc.
    ↓
Industry grows to meet demand for clothing, shoes, etc.
    → More wealth generated from taxes to pay for hotels, roads, airports, restaurants, etc.
```

What problems can tourism create?
- The profits from tourism 'leak out' of the local economy as payments to foreign-owned companies.
- The need to import foreign food and drink for the tourist palette may create a **trade deficit**.
- The jobs created tend to be confined to certain areas; people may migrate from other regions resulting in growing regional inequality.

The effects of economic change on the quality of life

- The so-called 'demonstration effect' (where hosts mimic tourist behaviour) may lead to begging, alcohol abuse and prostitution.
- Tourism can lead to the erosion of local customs and culture.
- The popularity of a resort can fade resulting in rapid economic decline.
- Tourism can cause environmental problems if not managed correctly.

Multinational companies

Many LEDCs attract foreign investment in the form of multinational companies. The impact of MNCs can be both positive and negative.

Know your case study

Freeport McMoRan, an American multinational company

Location The Freeport Copper mine at Grasberg, Irian Jaya (formerly West Papua New Guinea), Indonesia. The mine is the second largest copper mine in the world. 100,000 tonnes of ore are mined every day.

Benefits
- The company pays taxes to the Indonesian government for investment in the economy.
- The company supports the economy by purchasing local produce.
- The company employs over 6000 people in Indonesia.
- Incomes at the mine are above the national average.
- The company has invested in the infrastructure building roads and an airport.
- The company invests a percentage of profits into local-based development projects including housing and education and a new hospital.
- Employees receive free health care and education.

Problems
- The mine has inevitably caused environmental problems such as the destruction of the rainforest.
- 40 million tonnes of tailings (waste rock material) is dumped into the Ajewa River every year.
- The tailings result in acidification of waterways causing ecological damage and preventing use by local tribes.
- The Indonesian Transmigration scheme has resulted in the population increasing from a few hundred to several thousand. Most of the jobs are not taken by local people.
- The mine has disturbed the way of life of the Amungme and Kamoro tribes.
- The in-migration of Javanese has fuelled unrest between the Indonesian government and local people resulting in troops being brought in.
- The mining company is the single largest employer in the country and could decide to leave at any time with massive economic and social implications.

How can the development gap be closed?

Key Idea
- There are several alternative routes to development.

Key words and definitions

multinational company (MNC)	A company that operates in several countries.
aid	Money or assistance given by MEDCs to improve standards of living in LEDCs.
appropriate technology	Cheap, easily maintained technology which does not increase dependence on MEDCs for fuel or parts.

Hints and Tips!

Multinational companies locate in LEDCs to take advantage of cheap labour, and a non-unionized workforce. Multinational companies may improve standards of living locally but they take most of the profits out of the country.

Aid and development

Aid can be given in three ways:
1. **Non-Governmental Organizations (NGOs)** Groups such as Oxfam and Action Aid depend on voluntary contributions. Aid from these organizations is generally spent on small-scale 'bottom-up' community-based projects using appropriate technology.
2. **Bilateral Aid** This is aid given by one country to another country. Bilateral aid is often spent on 'top-down' developments such as large-scale building projects. Projects of this type are often unsuccessful, use inappropriate technology and can lead to debt problems. There is growing concern that governments give aid in return for trade agreements.
3. **Multilateral aid** This is aid given by countries via an international organization such as the World Bank or the UN. Individual countries cannot dictate what the money should be spent on.

Why is aid given?
- Many people feel that the MEDCs have a moral obligation to help those people less well off in LEDCs.
- Aid helps to build global solidarity.
- Aid can be mutually beneficial as it increases the spending power of the LEDCs which supports the export market and creates jobs in the MEDCs.
- Aid is often given for political reasons rather than humanitarian.

What problems can aid create?
- Aid can increase dependence on the MEDCs.
- Tied aid or boomerang aid is given in return for trade agreements that the LEDCs can ill afford.
- Aid can be misspent by governments and not reach those most in need.

Hints and Tips!
If you are asked to evaluate the success of a development project always discuss the benefits and the problems resulting from the scheme.

Know your case study

Top-down development
Location The dam is located on the River Pergau in Kelantan, a cultural region in the East of the Malaysian peninsula.
The scheme An HEP dam building project designed to provide 600 megawatts of electricity. The British government donated £234 million to the Malaysian government to help with the development. The scheme was designed to remove dependency on imported fossil fuels and reduce the trade deficit.

Success or failure?
- The dam has regulated the flow of the Pergau River, reducing flooding downstream.
- The aid was in the form of a low interest loan increasing the already substantial national debt to 97.5 million dollars.
- The dam caused the destruction of virgin rainforest.
- Large areas of land were flooded and many people were displaced.
- The river flow is unpredictable which makes HEP expensive.
- The Malaysian government signed a £1 billion arms agreement to buy arms from Britain to get the loan – money which could be better spent on social development.

Trade and investment

Key Idea
- The EU plays a central role in world trade. The patterns of trade associated with the EU help to shape the world economy.

Regional trade blocks

Primary products fetch low prices on the world market because of competition between LEDCs exporting the same goods. Countries cannot put their prices up as MEDCs would buy elsewhere. Some countries have increased their export revenue by creating trade blocks. The most successful example is OPEC which quadrupled the price of oil in the 1970s.

Trade and the EU

Know your case study

The EU currently has a population of 370 million. This makes it the biggest single market in the world. In 1992 the EU removed all internal trade barriers to encourage member countries to trade with each other. The EU has imposed tariffs on goods imported from outside the union, reducing competition from non-EU countries. As a result trade within the EU has increased. In fact, most EU countries conduct at least 50 per cent of their total trade with other EU members (75 per cent in Portugal).

There are also clear patterns of trade between the EU and non-member countries.
- The EU mainly exports manufactured goods with a high value on the world market.
- A significant percentage of exports are directed at non-EU countries in Europe because low transport costs make exports more attractive.
- Exports are also directed at other MEDCs such as the USA which have the purchasing power to buy expensive manufactured goods.
- There has been an increase in the percentage of exports to the NICs as their GDPs increase.
- Only a small percentage of exports go to the LEDCs.
- The EU mainly imports primary goods from LEDCs in Africa and Asia.
- The EU imports consumer products, such as electrical goods, from the USA and Japan.
- The UK maintains trade links with ex-colonies and the Commonwealth countries.

Membership of the EU offers countries many benefits. These include access to a massive market for their exports, a large, skilled workforce and protection from foreign competition. Many Eastern European countries have applied for EU membership. The level of economic and social development in Eastern Europe is much lower than the EU. Many issues must be considered when allowing new members to join:
- It would increase the size of the market.
- Low labour costs will result in cheaper goods being produced in Eastern Europe. Existing members may lose trade as countries begin importing more from the new members.
- The new members will need to be subsidized by the existing members. This would increase the amount of assistance given to existing periphery regions in need of development from the core regions.
- There may be migration of labour from the new members to other EU countries. This may cause unemployment in the more developed regions because there may not be enough jobs.

Unequal levels of development

Key Ideas
- The world can be divided roughly into the rich North and the poorer South.
- There are several ways to measure levels of development; some are better than others.

Key words and definitions

LEDC	Less economically developed country.
MEDC	More economically developed country.
GDP/GNP	The Gross Domestic Product/Gross National Product of a country is the amount of wealth generated by its economy. GDP does not include income from foreign investment.
indicator of development	Statistics that can be used as a measure of economic or social development.
human development index	A measure of social development derived from giving a score for real income, education and life expectancy.
informal sector	Employment which is not registered with the government for tax purposes.
NIC	Newly industialising country.

Hints and Tips!
Use the abbreviations LEDC and MEDC in the exam – they are recognized and it saves time.

Measuring economic development

The Brandt report, produced for the World Bank in the late 1970s, illustrated the global contrasts in **GDP**. It was noticed that the countries with higher GDP values were in the North and the countries with lower GDP values were in the South. However, GDP as a measure of national development is inadequate as it does not tell us about the distribution of wealth within the country. Nor does it tell us about standards of living in that country. In many **LEDC**s the GDP is not a true picture of economic activity within the country as many people work in the **informal sector** which will not appear in national statistics.

GDP can give us an idea of how economically developed a country is. However, some countries such as Saudi Arabia have a high GDP but a low standard of living as the wealth is not evenly distributed through society. Looking at standards of living in a country gives a better idea of levels of development than using GDP alone. Standards of living can be studied using a variety of indicators, as well as GDP, including:

Doctor/patient ratio This value shows how many patients there are for each doctor. This can be used to measure quality of health services. A high number of patients for each doctor suggests that health care is inadequate.

Life expectancy at birth A low life expectancy at birth indicates poor health care, poor diet, and a lack of sanitation.

Birth rate A high birth rate indicates lack of contraception, lack of education and a need for children to support the family financially.

Death rate A high death rate indicates poor diet, inadequate health care, and poor sanitation.

Adult literacy A low value suggests the population lacks education and incomes will be low.

Test Yourself

Themes
Give two reasons why GDP is not an ideal measure of development.

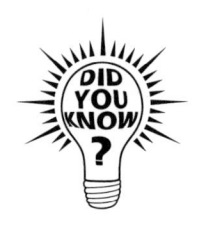

DID YOU KNOW?
85 per cent of the world's wealth is controlled by just 20 per cent of the population.

Unequal levels of development

Using any one of these indicators as the sole measure of development is unlikely to give you a reliable result. The best way to measure development is by using several indicators together in a development index.

The Human Development Index
This method used by the UN measures development using three indicators:
- **Purchasing power** What a certain amount of money can buy in different countries.
- **Educational attainment** The adult literacy rate and average number of years' schooling obtained.
- **Life expectancy at birth** To indicate quality of health care and diet.

The best conditions are given a score of one, the worst are given a score of zero. This system allows countries to be placed in relation to the most and least developed places. The HDI is a more flexible measure of development than GDP.

Test Yourself
Themes
Study the table of development indices. List the four LEDCs and give reasons for your choice.

Development indices of selected countries

	Japan	USA	UK	Italy	S.Korea	Brazil	India	Bangladesh
GNP (US $ per capita)	36,640	26,980	18,700	19,020	9,700	3,640	340	240
Life expectancy	77M 83F	73M 79F	74M 79F	75M 82F	70M 78F	57M 66F	60M 61F	56M 56F
Birth rate (per 1000)	10	15	13	10	16	20	25	30
Death rate (per 1000)	8	9	11	10	6	9	9	11
Infant mortality (per 1000 live births)	4	7	6	7	8	53	69	100
Adult literacy	99%	99%	99%	97%	97%	81%	50%	36%

It is important to remember that national averages give us only half the picture: within both MEDCs and LEDCs there are regional and local variations in quality of life. The regional variations tend to be greater in less developed countries, as does the gap between the richest and poorest in society. However it is important to remember that all LEDCs are different and avoid using stereotypes when describing them.

How and why do living standards vary?

Key Ideas
- Unfair terms of trade make the rich richer and the poor poorer.
- There are many explanations for the differences in the level of development between MEDCs and LEDCs.

Key words and definitions
trade	The exchange of goods and services in return for money.
exports	Goods sold by a country.
imports	Goods bought by a country.
trade deficit	When the value of imports exceeds the value of exports.
tariffs	Taxes imposed on foreign imports making them more expensive therefore encouraging people to buy home-produced goods.

Hints and Tips!
If you are provided in the exam with statistics like these in the table try to quote them in your answer. A specific response, which uses the resource, will gain more marks than a general comment.

Economic systems and development

Some of the reasons why living standards in LEDCs remain low include:

1. **Colonialism and dependency** Many LEDCs used to be colonies of the industrialized countries. MEDCs used the raw materials from the colonies to industrialize and prevented the colonies from developing manufacturing industries of their own. During this era of colonialism the LEDCs became dependent on the export of primary products to the MEDCs.

2. **Tied down by trade** The pattern of world trade keeps less developed countries poor because:
   - the LEDCs export cheap primary products and import expensive manufactured goods from the MEDCs. This pattern of trade results in unequal levels of development as the less developed countries spend much more on **imports** than they earn from **exports**
   - the value of primary goods on the world market is unpredictable as supplies vary from year to year
   - over time, the real value of primary goods has fallen, while the cost of manufactured goods has continued to rise. This creates a **trade deficit** that means there is less money to invest in health care, education and the economy.

The balance of trade – countries exporting raw materials

Country	Value of exports	Commodities	Value of imports	Commodities
Ghana	$1.57 billion	Gold 39% Cocoa beans 35% Timber 9.4%	$1.84 billion	Machinery, petroleum, foodstuffs
Niger	$188 million	Uranium ore 67% Livestock (meat) 20%	$374 million	Machinery, vehicle parts, petroleum
Sudan	$620 million	Cotton 23% Sesame 22% Livestock 13% Gum 5%	$1.5 billion	Food, petroleum, manufactured goods, machinery, medicines
Zambia	$2.5 billion	Agricultural goods 38% Gold 12% Other metals 7% Textiles 4%	$2.2 billion	Machinery, manufactured goods, chemicals

3. **Protectionism** Many MEDCs have put **tariffs** on manufactured imports from less developed countries. This protects their own industries while making it difficult for LEDCs to develop by exporting manufactured goods.

4. **Debt** When interest rates were low in the 1970s, many LEDCs took out loans. The loans were spent on developing infrastructure and the economy. However, the interest rates went up leaving many LEDCs owing more than they originally borrowed. This debt burden reduces the country's GDP significantly.

Top four debtor countries	
Brazil	US$ 179 billion
Mexico	US$ 157.1 billion
Indonesia	US$ 129 billion
China	US$ 128.8 billion

Exam practice – higher level paper

B6 This question is about Economic Systems and Development.

Study the table below.

Country	GNP (US $) 1980	GNP (US $) 1996
USA	9,590	25,860
Japan	7,280	34,630
UK	5,030	18,410
Italy	3,850	19,270
Brazil	1,570	3,370
South Korea	1,510	8,220
Nigeria	560	280
Indonesia	360	880
China	230	530
Burkina Faso	160	300

(a) (i) Which country was least successful in improving its GNP between 1980 and 1996?

    (ii) Which country was changing most rapidly from having a less developed to having a more developed economy? [2]

(b) Suggest three headings you could use to divide the countries in the table on the basis of their changing GNP. [2]

(c) Suggest two reasons why some countries, like some of those in the table, have been able to develop their economies more rapidly than others. [4]

(d) The use of GNP is one way of measuring development.

    (i) Suggest two other measures that could be used.

    (ii) Justify the measures you have suggested. Include any reservations you may have about their use. [4]

(e) In some places economic activity is growing while in others it is declining. For a country or region you have studied:

    (i) name and locate the country or region

    (ii) explain the main changes in economic activity

    (iii) describe the impact these changes are having on the quality of life. [8]

[Total 20 marks]

Summary

Economic systems and development

Theme 3 check list

	Confident	Not bad	Needs more work
Economic systems			
I know the four sectors of the economy	☐	☐	☐
I can explain economic activity as a system	☐	☐	☐
I know at least five factors that affect the location of different types of economic activity	☐	☐	☐
Economic activity, growth and change			
I can explain how developments in transport have resulted in changes in economic activity	☐	☐	☐
I know how developments in technology have affected economic activity	☐	☐	☐
I know the impact of change over time on location for an economic activity	☐	☐	☐
I know why some places grow economically while other places decline	☐	☐	☐
I know how tourism can affect economic development in an LEDC	☐	☐	☐
I know what multinational corporations are and how they affect economic development in an LEDC	☐	☐	☐
I know how a development project can affect economic development in an LEDC	☐	☐	☐
I know about economic change within regions of the EU	☐	☐	☐
I know how quality of life varies between regions because of economic change	☐	☐	☐
International disparities, trade and interdependence			
I know about different levels of development in the world	☐	☐	☐
I know six indicators that can be used to measure contrasts in living standards	☐	☐	☐
I know how investment and aid can improve the quality of life in LEDCs	☐	☐	☐
I understand the general pattern of world trade	☐	☐	☐
I can explain what is meant by interdependence	☐	☐	☐
I can describe trade, investment and aid links between different countries	☐	☐	☐

Test Yourself

Tick the boxes – if you still do not understand seek help from your teacher.

Summary

Test Yourself

Themes

What examples have you studied?

Primary industry: _____

Secondary industry: _____

Tertiary industry: _____

Quaternary industry: _____

Hints and Tips!
Write down the names of your chosen case studies. Ask your teacher to check your choices.

Know your case studies

Which real places have you studied as an example of:
- an economic system   name and location _____
- transport and technology developments in
   industry in an MEDC   name and location _____
- transport and technology developments in
   industry in the EU   name and location _____
- economic change in an MEDC (not the EU)   name and location _____
- economic change in the EU   name and location _____
- economic development in an LEDC   name and location _____
- investment or an aid programme in an LEDC   name and location _____
- EU trade   name and location _____

Theme 4: Population and settlement

For this theme you will need to know about:
- population distribution, structure and change
- the effects of birth rates, death rates and migration and its impact on population, structure and change
- the location and function of settlements
- the growth and decline of settlements.

Key Idea
- People are not evenly spread out. Some places have a dense population; some have a sparse population.

Key words and definitions
population density   The number of people per square km
dense   Many people per square km.
sparse   Few people per square km.
distribution   How people are spread out.

Population distribution

The map below shows the global distribution of population. Points to note:
- areas north of the Arctic Circle are sparsely populated
- the most densely populated areas are generally in the northern hemisphere.
- the two most densely populated regions are Europe and Asia.

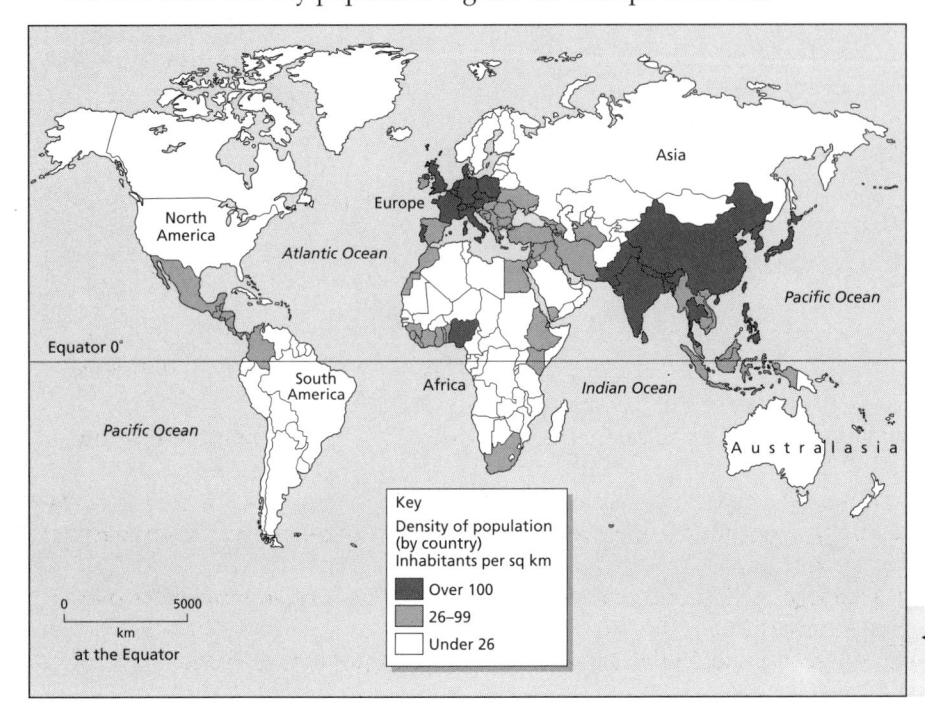

Test Yourself

Places

1. Use an atlas to identify two countries which are sparsely populated, and two that are densely populated.

2. For both a densely and sparsely poulated country you have identified, list reasons for the density of population. One country should be an MEDC and one should be an LEDC.

◀ World population distribution

Population distribution

Population density and distribution are affected by a number of environmental and human factors. Factors which lead to a dense population are called positive factors. Factors which lead to a sparse population are called negative factors.

Positive factors	Negative factors
Fertile soils	Infertile soils
Reliable water supply	Unreliable water supply
Moderate climate	Extreme climate
Flat land	Steep slopes and mountains
Raw materials	Lack of raw materials
Good communications	Lack of communications
Political stability	Political instability

Hints and Tips!

Not all these factors apply to a single place and there are exceptions to them, for instance some of the hottest desert areas have pockets of dense population due to their mineral resources.

Know your case study

The population distribution of Japan, an MEDC

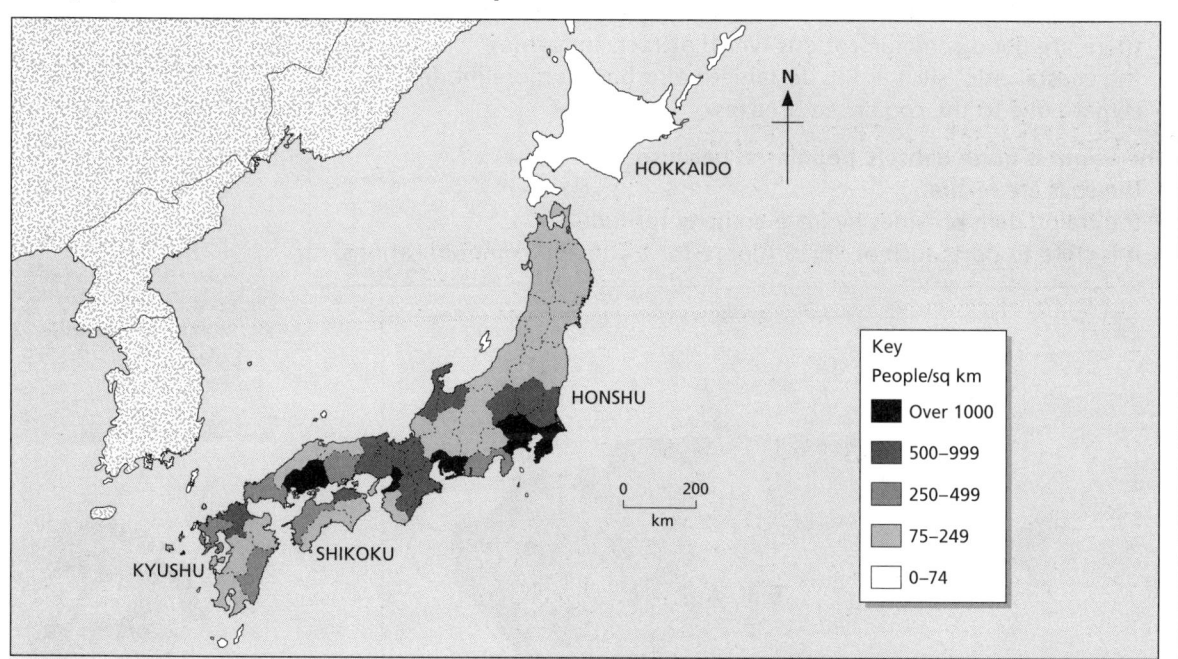

▲ *Population distribution of Japan*

- The northern island of Hokkaido is quite sparsely populated because it is mountainous and the slopes are densely forested. It is also much colder than the rest of Japan.
- The main island of Honshu has an uneven population distribution. The south coast is very densely populated with over 1000 people per square km in some parts. This is because the Pacific coastal plain offers flat land and fertile soils.
- The interior of Honshu is sparsely populated because it is dominated by rugged mountains over 3000m high and is relatively inaccessible.
- The two southern islands of Kyushu and Shikoku have a moderate population density.

Population and settlement

Know your case study

The population distribution of Brazil, an LEDC

The North is very sparsely populated because:
- most is covered in impenetrable rainforest of the Amazonian Basin
- the climate is very wet and hot (average monthly rainfall of 60mm)
- the soils are infertile and unsuitable for commercial cultivation
- there are small pockets of higher density population surrounding mineral exploitation schemes such as Carajas.

The Centre West is quite sparsely populated because:
- it is dominated by low plateaux and grassland and is hot and dry
- the Mato Grosso, a grassland, is unsuitable for productive agriculture.

The North East is moderately populated because:
- there are many ports on the coast, which generate trade, e.g. Recife
- the area has many sugar and palm oil plantations providing employment.

However, the area is suffering from drought and the population density may decrease as people migrate to more productive areas.

The South East is very densely populated because:
- the area is rich in minerals such as iron ore and bauxite which attract industries
- the soils are fertile and good for agriculture e.g. coffee plantations
- there are good communications which attracts industries
- the coastal cities such as Rio de Janiero also have a more moderate climate due to the cooler sea breezes.

The South is quite densely populated because:
- the soils are fertile
- the Itaipu dam provides hydro-electricity for industry
- it is close to ports such as Porto Alegre for trade and communications.

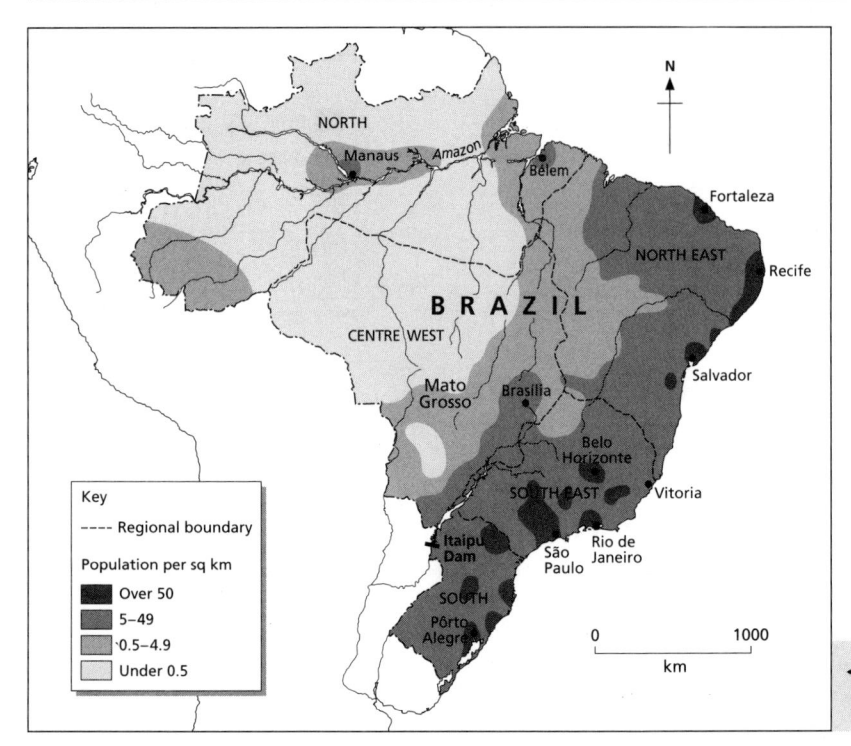

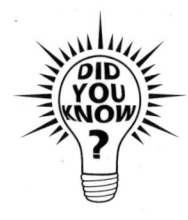

DID YOU KNOW?

If you subtract the oceans we are left with 25 per cent of the Earth's surface on which to live. Take away the deserts and drought-stricken regions, the mountains, lakes and rivers, the polar ice caps and permafrost we are left with just 11 per cent of the land's surface for human habitation!

Hints and Tips!

Explaining population distributions is quite simple, just try to consider the relief, climate, communications and raw materials, and you can probably suggest whether a place will be densely or sparsely populated.

Test Yourself

Places

Try to spot the reasons for population distribution on the map of Brazil.

◀ Population distribution of Brazil

Key
- ---- Regional boundary
- Population per sq km
  - Over 50
  - 5–49
  - 0.5–4.9
  - Under 0.5

Population structure

Key words and definitions

population structure	The composition of a population in terms of age groups and gender.
birth rate	The number of babies born per 1000 people.
child dependents	People under the age of 16 (14 in most LEDCs).
death rate	The number of people dying for every 1000 people.
dependency ratio	The number of dependents for every economically active person.
economically active	People of working age (16-65 years in UK).
elderly dependents	People over 65 years (pensioners).
infant mortality	Death of children under the age of 1 year.
life expectancy	The average length of life.

Interpreting a population pyramid

A population pyramid is a graph to show the population structure of a place. Reading these graphs is easy if you know what you are looking for:
- the higher the graph, the higher the **life expectancy**
- if the two sides are unequal there is a gender imbalance usually caused by war or migration
- if the base of the graph is wide it suggests that there is a high **birth rate** and high percentage of child dependents
- if the top of the graph narrows quickly there is a low **life expectancy** and a small percentage of elderly and dependents.

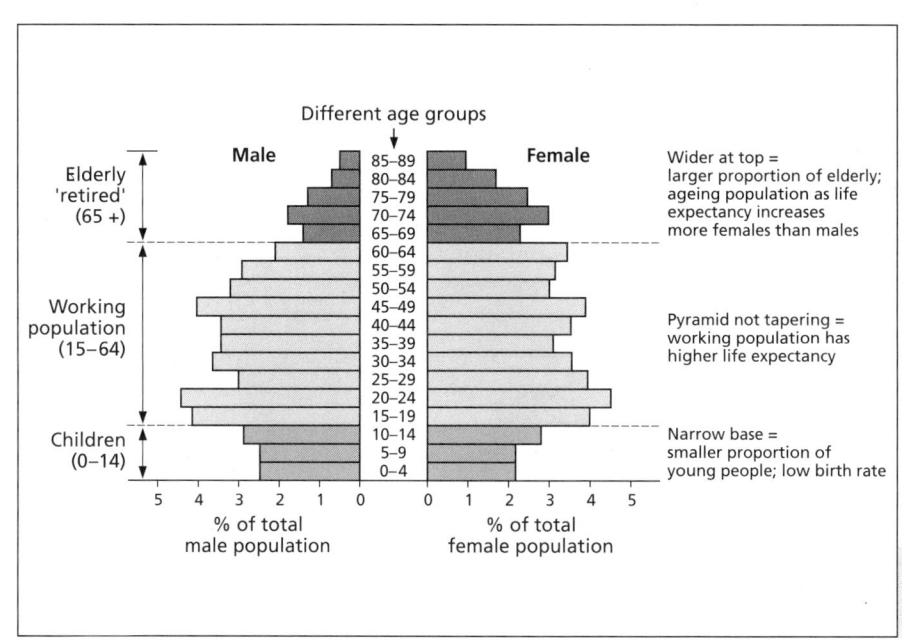

Test Yourself

Places

1. For an MEDC you have studied, what percentage of the population is classed as dependent?

2. What percentage of the population is classed as **economically active**?

3. Now divide the percentage of dependents by the percentage of economically active to calculate the **dependency ratio**.

◀ *Population pyramid for France*

Population and settlement

Population change and levels of development

Population change can be studied using the Demographic Transition Model, which shows how birth and death rates change as a country develops.

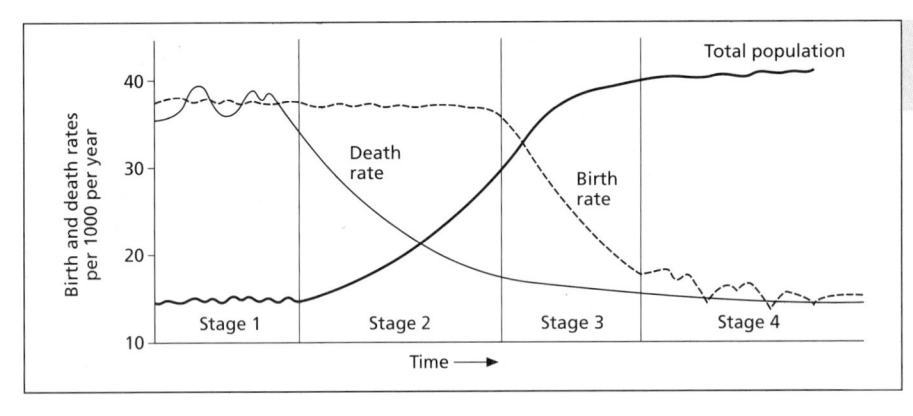

◀ *The demographic transition model*

Stage 2

Countries in stage two include LEDCs such as Kenya and India. Pyamids for this stage tend to be wide at the base and narrow quickly. They have a large number of child dependents as birth rates are high. Families tend to be large as children can help to support the family from an early age. Many people live in remote rural areas and do not have access to contraception and family planning. **Infant mortality** rates are high and people depend on their children in old age. As a result people have large numbers of children to ensure some survive to adulthood. The pyramid narrows quickly indicating low life expectancy. Death rates are falling however due to improvements in health care and sanitation. As many more people are born than are dying the population increases rapidly.

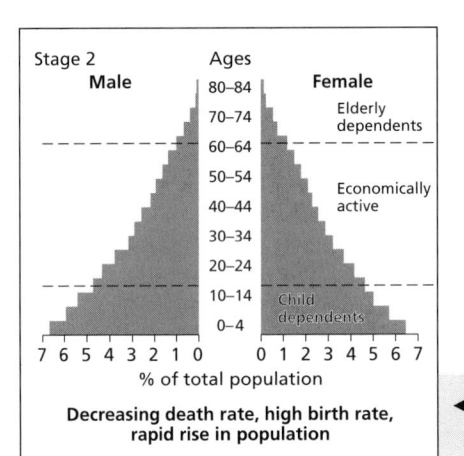

◀ *Population pyramid for stage 2*

Stage 4

Countries in stage four of the model include MEDCs such as the UK, the USA and Japan. Pyramids for this stage tend to be more oval shaped than pyramidal as the base is narrow, while the middle age groups are more uniform. Here the death rates have fallen as a result of medical advances and are now very low. However, birth rates are also low. The birth rates in MEDCs are low due to higher incomes and a better standard of living. Attitudes towards children have changed; they are no longer needed to support the family and having children may actually reduce the standard of living. Contraception and family planning are widely available. As birth and death rates are more or less equal the population remains steady.

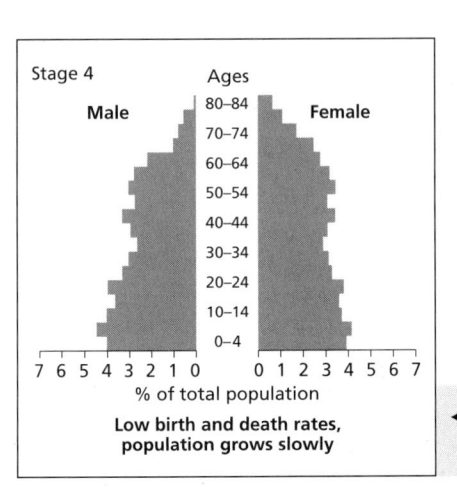

◀ *Population pyramid for stage 4*

Test Yourself

Themes

1. Describe three differences between stage 2 and 4 population pyramids
2. Give clear reasons to explain each difference.

Hints and Tips!

An LEDC will usually have a higher dependency ratio than an MEDC. This is due to high numbers of **child dependents** and a low life expectancy leading to fewer economically active people.

Population change

Key Ideas
- Populations may increase and decrease over time.
- Population change may be due to the balance of births and deaths or to migration; often it is a combination of both.

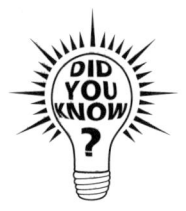

Key words and definitions
natural increase — The birth rate minus the death rate, or the difference between the birth rate and death rate.

Natural increase

Natural increase is the balance between births and deaths. This balance will change in response to many factors. Some of these are illustrated in the diagram below.

High Birth rate ← Low
- Lack of education
- Low status of women
- Religion and tradition
- High infant mortality
- Low incomes
- Lack of contraception
- Government policy

High Death rate ← Low
- Lack of health care
- Inadequate diet
- Lack of clean water
- Poor sanitation
- War

Low Birth rate
- Government policy
- High incomes
- Family planning and contraception
- Higher status of women
- Low infant mortality
- Child labour laws
- Education

Low Death rate
- Medical progress
- Sanitation
- Clean water supply
- Peace
- Good diet

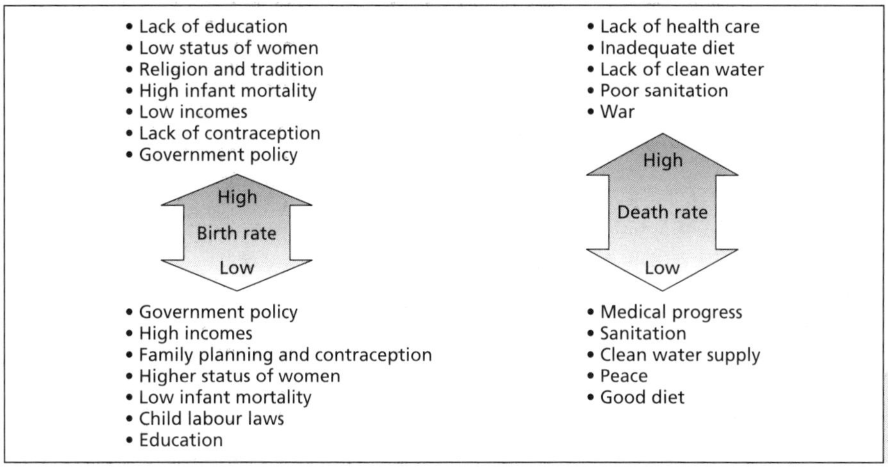

◀ *Factors affecting birth and death rates*

Did You Know?
Every second three people are born and two people die, so the population of the world increases by one!

Hints and Tips!
If the birth rate is 11 and the death rate is 7, the natural increase will be 4. However, if the death rate is greater than the birth rate you will get a negative number. This shows that the population is decreasing.

Natural increase is usually higher in LEDCs than in MEDCs. This is because LEDCs tend to have high birth rates and falling death rates so the difference between them is growing. MEDCs tend to have low birth rates and low death rates with little difference between them.

Test Yourself

Themes

1. Using the graph:
   - give the decade with the greatest natural increase
   - give the birth and death rates for 1990
   - calculate the rate of natural increase in 1990
   - decide what has happened to the rate of natural increase since 1960.
2. Complete the table opposite to summarize the Demographic Transition Model (page 84).
3. Give three reasons birth rates are high in LEDCs.
4. Give three reasons birth rates are low in MEDCs.
5. Give three reasons why death rates fall as a country develops.

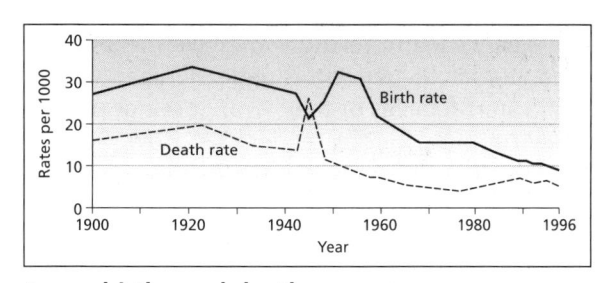

Japan births and deaths

Summary of demographic model

	Stage 1	Stage 2	Stage 3	Stage 4
Birth rate	High			Low
Death rate		Falling		Low
Population change				

Coping with population change

Population change can have a massive impact on a place's economy and society. An increasing population means there will be more competition for jobs, housing, and food. In severe cases overpopulation can lead to starvation, homelessness and war. A decreasing population on the other hand may lead to a shortage of workers.

> **Know your case study**
>
> ### Iran, controlling population growth in an LEDC
>
> **Population change**
> - Since the 1979 revolution the population of Iran has increased by 25 million people.
> - People were encouraged to have large families to increase the Islamic population.
> - The revolutionary government felt under threat from external forces such as Iraq.
> - The legal age for marriage was reduced to 9 years. Television and radio broadcasts encouraged people to have more children.
> - The government closed family planning clinics.
>
> **Effects of population change**
> Throughout the 1980s the government was becoming increasingly worried about the effect the growth rate would have on the provision of education, health care and employment. Fears of declining standards of living prompted action in 1993.
>
> **Controlling the population growth**
> In 1993 the government passed new family planning laws:
> - Free contraception was made widely available.
> - Government-funded vasectomy clinics were opened.
> - Couples hoping to marry are required to attend an hour-long lecture on family planning.
> - Cheap health insurance and food coupons were abolished for the fourth and subsequent children.
>
> **The effect**
> It is very early to tell how effective these measures will be. Of the population 45 per cent is under 17 years of age and they will grow up and start families of their own. It seems probable that the growth rate will continue for several decades. However, Iran has taken action sooner rather than later to try to prevent overpopulation.

Test Yourself

Places

1. For Iran, or another LEDC you have studied, list four measures taken to control population growth.
2. Why is population growth such an important issue for LEDCs?

Hints and Tips!

Overpopulation is when the number of people exceeds the availability of resources. It can result in starvation, war or disease. Some people believe technology will overcome the problems of food supply.

Effects of population change in MEDCs

In MEDCs the main problem concerning population is an increase in the percentage of elderly dependents. The UK, Germany and Japan are experiencing this 'greying' process.

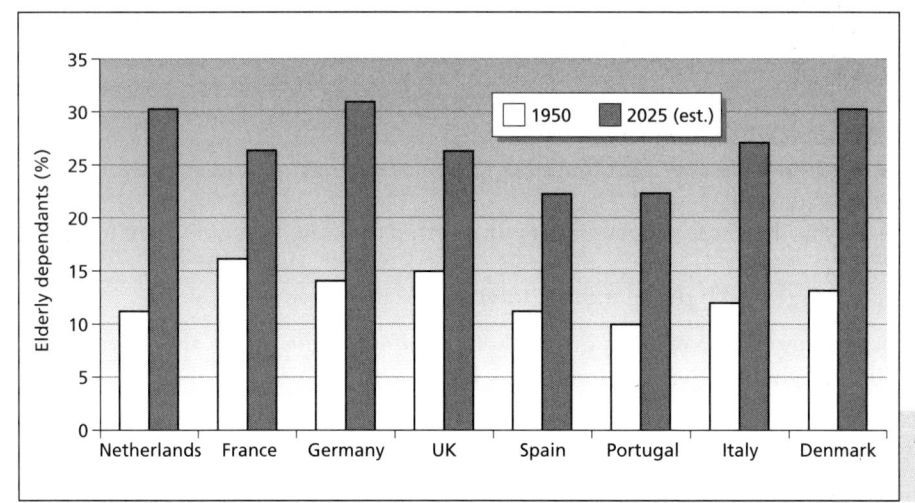

◀ *Increase in percentage of elderly in the EU*

Summary

Populations in LEDCs have:
- high birth rates
- falling death rates
- rapid natural increase
- a high dependency ratio.

Populations in MEDCs have:
- low birth rates
- low death rates
- stable or declining populations
- a lower dependency ratio.

Hints and Tips!

Spain, Portugal and southern Italy will experience slower growth in the percentage of elderly because they are in the economic periphery of the EU. Lower standards of living mean that life expectancy will be lower than in the more wealthy core countries.

Themes

1. Which EU country had the highest percentage of elderly in 1950?
2. Which EU country will experience the most rapid increase in the percentage of elderly by 2025?

Places

1. From your study of the EU identify one country where population is changing.
2. Describe the change taking place.
3. Explain why the population is changing.

Migration

Key Ideas
- People migrate due to a combination of push and pull factors.
- Migration affects the population of the origin and the destination.

Key words and definitions

migration	When people move permanently from one place to another. It can be internal, within a country, or external, to and from a country.
push factors	Conditions in the home area (origin) that make people feel they should move to improve their quality of life.
pull factors	Opportunities in another area (destination) which attract people to move there for a better life.
urbanization	A growing percentage of the population in towns and cities.

There are many different types of migration. You can group them in terms of the origin and destination, e.g. rural to urban, or according to whether they are temporary or permanent. You can also classify them as forced or voluntary migrations.

Types of migration

Rural to urban	From countryside to urban settlements.
Urban to rural	From urban areas to the countryside.
Urban to urban	Movement between urban areas.
Rural to rural	From one rural place to another.
International	A migration which crosses a national boundary into another country.
Internal	A migration within a country, from one region to another.

Push factors	Pull factors
Lack of job opportunities, e.g. • in remote rural areas • in former coal mining areas • in textile and pottery areas • in shipbuilding, iron and steel.	Job opportunities, e.g. • in tourist honeypots • in IT industries • in service industries • in new car assembly plants
Poor housing, e.g. in inner city areas	Housing, e.g. houses with gardens
Poor environment, e.g. crime, noise, pollution, traffic	Safety, privacy, green areas
War and civil strife	Political stability
Poor schools	Quality schools and educational opportunity
Lack of health care	Provision of health care for young and elderly
Increased wealth and car purchase	Opportunities to use wealth to improve quality of life, e.g. home with garage, golf club
Age, e.g. new workers and recently retired	Age, e.g. people with similar social habits
Family breakdown, e.g. divorce	Presence of family and friends
Personal restlessness	Desire for new experiences
Loss of sense of community	Recognition of sense of community

Migration

Know your case study

The pull of the EU
The EU countries are wealthy and have good standards of living. This cannot be said for all European countries. The Eastern European countries, such as Poland, are much less developed. Many people try to cross illegally into the EU in hope of a better life.

Push factors
Poland is a very poor country when compared to those in the EU. GDP per capita is only $3500. The unemployment rate is over 11 per cent. Incomes are low and standards of living are poor resulting in poor health and high infant mortality.

Pull factors
The EU countries, such as Germany and other core regions, offer factory work and much higher incomes. Education and health care and good quality housing are all factors which attract migrants from Eastern Europe.

Illegal entry
Migrants enter Germany by crossing the River Oder. It is not known exactly how many people have crossed the border but it is thought to be thousands. The illegal immigrants are mainly Polish or Romanians seeking employment. The immigrants pay smugglers up to $1000 each to be taken across the border. Most immigrants find work on farms or in cities such as Berlin on construction sites, bars and hotels.

The effect
The EU has approximately three million illegal workers. The migrants are often willing to work for lower wages than the nationals. People resent the competition for jobs. In many areas there has been an increase in racism as people blame the immigrants for unemployment. Germany has very strict immigration laws to control the flow of migrants.

Hints and Tips!
When discussing the causes of a migration always include push and pull factors.

Test Yourself — Themes
Give three push and three pull factors associated with the type of migration in this case study.

Rural to urban migration and urbanization

Key Ideas
- It is the movement of people from rural areas to the cities which causes rapid urbanization in LEDCs.
- Rapid growth of cities can cause economic and social problems.

> **Did you know?** In 1930 the population of São Paulo was only one million, now it is over 17 million and still growing!

Know your case study

Rural to urban migration in Brazil, an LEDC

Origin of migrants
The agricultural regions of the North East surrounding the Rio Ceara and Rio Moco. Small plantation settlements such as Murupai in the sugar plantation region.

Push factors
- The economy is dominated by agriculture and incomes are low.
- Agriculture is dominated by large landowners that evict tenant farmers with little warning.
- The area has suffered from twelve major droughts in this century alone.
- Soils are poor and low productivity keeps incomes down.
- Villages lack basic services such as schools and health centres.
- Many houses are without water and drainage.

Destination
The cities of the South East such as São Paulo and Belo Horizonte.

Pull factors
- Employment in factories such as Fiat and Volkswagen offer higher wages.
- Access to schools and health care.
- Better standard of housing with water and power supplied by authorities.

The effects of the migration to São Paulo
- Over six million people have moved to the city of São Paulo in the last ten years.
- The economic growth has not kept pace with the growth of population and millions live in poverty.
- There is a massive shortage of housing; over six million people live in self-built or temporary dwellings.
- Six areas of squatter settlements or *favelas* have developed on the *peripheria* (edge of town). These *favelas* are often illegal and lack sufficient mains water and power supplies.
- Urban poverty is increasing and standards of living are falling; infant mortality has doubled in the last ten years. Villa Prudenté is one such area of housing.
- There are not enough manufacturing jobs. Unemployment is not an option as there are no benefits. A thriving informal economy has developed where millions of people earn money through informal jobs in the *favelas* such as mechanics, cleaners, and dressmakers. However, these workers do not pay tax and the government struggles to pay for essential services.

Know your case study

Coping with rapid urbanization in LEDCs
There are many ways of dealing with the growth of squatter settlements. Some approaches are more successful than others.

1 Large-scale housing projects: The city of Caracas in Venezuela
- The government built 'super blocks' – cheap, prefabricated blocks of high-rise flats.
- Each flat cost $10,000 and was offered for rent in order to cover the cost of construction.
- The flats proved expensive to repair and maintain.
- 50 per cent of tenants could not afford the rents.
- Flats were sub-let and became dangerously overcrowded.
- The flats attracted more migrants to the city and squatter settlements developed around the flats.

2 Site and service schemes: Arrumbakam, Madras in India
Indian planners realized they could not stop the arrival of migrants. They decided that the best way to improve services in urban areas was to install them before the migrants settled.
- Over 13,000 building plots were prepared.
- Each plot was connected to water, drainage and electricity.
- The plots were offered for sale, providing an incentive to improve the dwellings.
- Cheap building materials were available locally.
- Small workshops were built to generate employment and income for local people.
- People improved the dwellings gradually as and when they could afford to buy materials.
- Unfortunately 40 per cent of the population were not paying taxes and the government cannot afford to maintain this policy forever.

3 Shanty town improvement schemes: Villa Prudente in São Paulo, Brazil
- The government invested in street lighting, sanitation and water supplies in an attempt to improve living conditions in the favelas.
- Roads were surfaced and refuse collection points arranged.
- Recession in the late 1980s resulted in a cut in spending – new improvement schemes were not planned.

4 Rural development schemes: Kerala in southern India
- Government recognized that the best way of preventing urban poverty was to improve life in the rural areas.
- The Community Development Society is an organization of nearly 400,000 women. With the support of government and UNICEF the CDS set up anti-poverty schemes in 57 rural settlements.
- Funds were made available for literacy schemes, provision of water supplies and basic latrines, and health care. Villagers were encouraged to establish kitchen gardens to improve diet and nutrition.
- Schemes like this improve the quality of life in rural areas and reduce the need for migration. However, funding these schemes is difficult and rural areas will still lag behind urban areas in many ways.

Hints and Tips!
Improving urban areas often only serves to attract more migrants from rural areas.

Population and settlement

① A migration within the EU _____

Push	Pull	Effect on origin	Effect on destination

② A migration between countries outside the EU _____

Push	Pull	Effect on origin	Effect on destination

③ Rural-urban migration in an LEDC _____

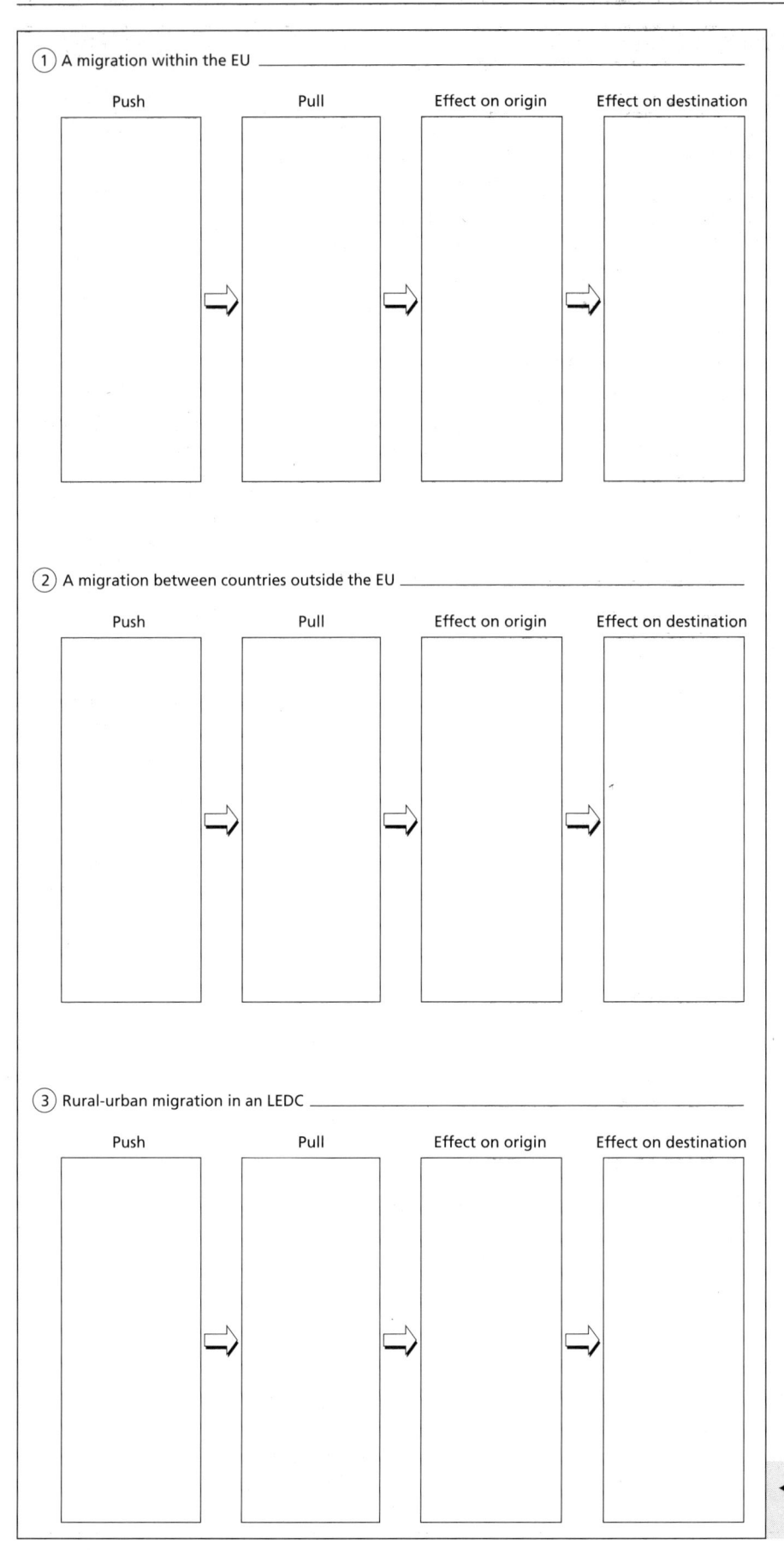

Push	Pull	Effect on origin	Effect on destination

Test Yourself

Places

Using either rural to urban migration in Brazil or another example you have studied, complete the summary diagram opposite.

◀ *Migration summary diagram*

The location of settlements

The origin of settlements

Historically settlement locations were chosen because they offered either good defence, access to raw materials and daily needs such as food and water, or to trade routes. Typical sites for settlements include:

1. **A river loop or meander site** Settlements were built inside a meander which acted as a natural moat. Water was readily available but the site might suffer from flooding, e.g. Warkworth.
2. **A dry point site** In marshy areas prone to flooding settlements were located on areas of higher land.
3. **A hilltop site** In periods of war settlements were located on hilltops as they offered a good viewpoint and were easily defended.
4. **A crossroads site** Settlements located at a crossroads were ideally placed to take advantage of passing trade and were accessible from all directions.
5. **A ford or bridging point** Settlements were often located at a river crossing to take advantage of traders passing through.
6. **A gap site** A gap in a range of hills was often chosen as a good location. Traders would use the gap as a trade route; the settlement could control the use of the gap and the hills offered shelter.
7. **A spring line settlement** In limestone areas settlements were often located along the spring line for access to a water supply.

Test Yourself — Themes

Cover the page and see how many of the typical settlement sites you can remember.

Hints and Tips!

When describing the location of a settlement think of its position in relation to the surroundings, including other settlements, roads, rivers, landmarks and the position within the region.

▼ *Settlement sites*

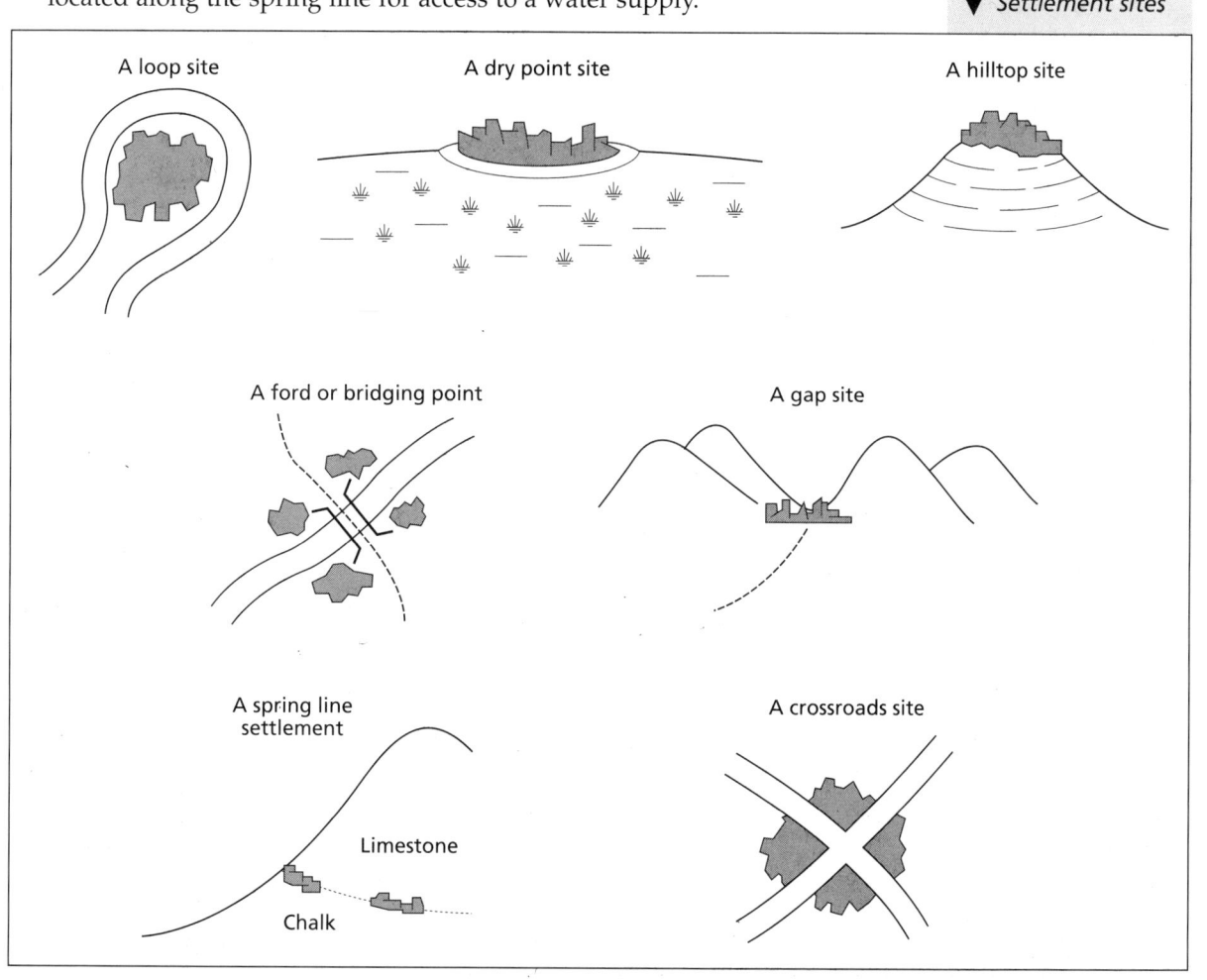

The settlement hierarchy

Key Ideas
- There are different types of settlement which differ in terms of size, population and function.
- Settlements are organized in a hierarchy according to size and function.

Key words and definitions

sphere of influence/ hinterland	The region from which a settlement can attract people.
function	The type of services offered by a settlement.
high order	Goods or services that are expensive or used infrequently.
low order	Goods or services that are inexpensive and used frequently.
range	The distance from which people are willing to travel.
threshold population	The number of people needed to support a particular function.

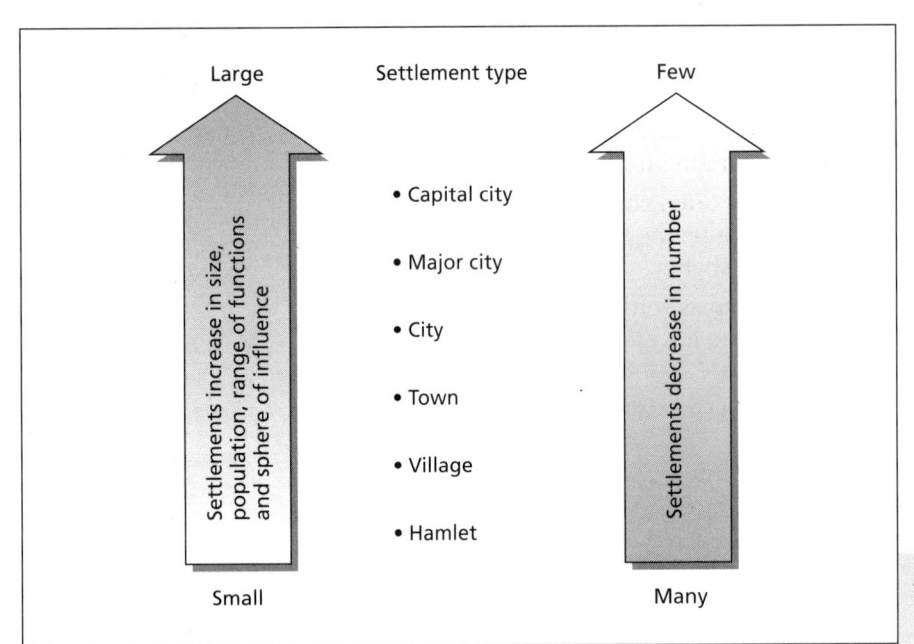

Settlement type (Large → Small; Few → Many):
- Capital city
- Major city
- City
- Town
- Village
- Hamlet

Settlements increase in size, population, range of functions and sphere of influence.
Settlements decrease in number.

◀ *The settlement hierarchy*

Test Yourself

Places

Use your knowledge of your own region, or one you have studied, to name a settlement in each of the levels of the hierarchy.

Are settlement size, function and location linked?

Any urban region will have a city surrounded by several smaller towns and many smaller villages.

The villages will have only a few functions such as a post office and village shop selling inexpensive everyday goods such as bread and milk. People are not willing to travel far for cheap everyday goods and village shops have a small **sphere of influence**. People in villages will travel to the town for things like weekly groceries. For more expensive goods or higher order services villagers will take a longer trip to the city.

The towns have a larger population and can support a wider range of services. Towns tend to have more **low order** and middle order **functions** and shops to which people are willing to travel moderate distances. People will travel to the city for more expensive, **high order** goods.

The city has a very large population and can support a large range of functions including high order functions such as furniture shops and department stores, and hospitals. People are willing to travel long distances for high order services as they are expensive or used infrequently. Cities attract people from a wide area and have a large sphere of influence.

Hints and Tips!
When deciding where to shop people will consider the distance to travel and transport costs, the value of the goods, how often the trip will be needed and the range of functions available at different settlements.

Declining settlements

Key Ideas
- Settlements are dynamic places that are constantly changing.
- People and services have begun to leave large urban areas moving to smaller settlements in rural areas.

Key words and definitions

deurbanization (or counterurbanization)	The migration of people and services from the cities to the countryside.
deindustrialization	The decline of traditional industries.
urban regeneration	Schemes to generate employment in and improve the environment of inner-city areas.

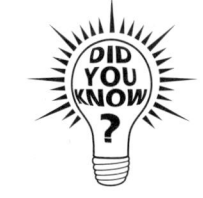

Deurbanization

Unlike LEDCs, many cities in more developed countries are experiencing a decline in population. This process of **deurbanization** is linked closely to the relocation of industry and services. Many of the traditional industries such as steel and textiles have declined since the 1960s. The industry that has survived is opting out of the inner city in favour of new locations on the urban–rural fringe.

Did you know? Currys have closed over 40 city centre outlets and opened new out-of-town superstores instead!

✗ Negative factors of inner city	✔ Positive factors of out-of-town locations
Old premises unsuitable for modern production techniques	New modern premises can be built to house modern technology
Lack of space for expansion	More space available for expansion and parking
Narrow grid layout of roads unsuitable for lorries	Closer to motorway junctions for improved access
High crime rates increase security costs	Closer to skilled workforce in the suburbs
Congestion increases delivery times	Less congestion
Pollution and decaying environment	A cleaner, quieter environment
Expensive land prices	Cheaper land reduces overheads

Problems associated with decline of settlements

The out-migration of people and industry has left many inner urban areas suffering from economic and social decline. In Birmingham, unemployment was more than 30 per cent in some inner city districts such as Aston, Sparkbrook and Handsworth. Quality of life in the inner cities was much lower than the national average. The government invested in several schemes to regenerate the inner urban areas. The schemes include: The Urban Programme, Enterprize Zones, Urban Development Corporations and City Challenge.

Growth of rural settlements

Key Idea
- Deurbanization also affects the rural villages that have to cope with new arrivals. Villages that are close to major cities are more popular than villages in remote agricultural regions.

Key words and definitions

dormitory villages   Villages where the majority of residents sleep at night while spending the days working in the city.

green belt   A zone around the outside of a city in which new building is strictly regulated by town planners.

The effect of deurbanization on rural villages:
- The population increases so new homes must be built which often changes the traditional character of the village.
- The demand for property pushes up house prices forcing many locals to move out.
- The larger population can support new services such as secondary schools.
- The commuters own cars and so rural bus services are cut.
- New residents shop in the city causing local shops to close.
- There is often friction between locals and the 'comers-in'.
- Rural roads become congested and noisy.

These changes are happening all over the UK as people are lured to the countryside by dreams of life in a peaceful village. Unfortunately, by following their dreams people are destroying the rural qualities they are seeking. Many new housing estates boast names such as 'The Meadows' or 'The Oaks' as reminders of what used to be found there. In an attempt to prevent the erosion of green areas around major cities councils created **green belts**.

Hints and Tips!
The arrival of new people from the cities can cause problems for rural villages as well as breathe life back into them.

Hints and Tips!
You should know an example of settlement growth or decline in an LEDC and from an EU country.

Know your case study

Bishops Cleeve – A growing settlement in the EU

Location
Bishops Cleeve is a former village approximately 3 miles north of Cheltenham in Gloucestershire. The settlement lies at the foot of Cleeve Hill in the Cotswolds, and is linked to the town of Cheltenham by the A435. The M5 runs 2 miles to the west.

Settlement Change
- Bishop's Cleeve has steadily grown in size to its present population of 4000 habitants.
- The growth is predominantly due to counter urbanisation, as people seek a rural/semi-rural residential alternative to the town of Cheltenham.
- Improvements in personal mobility make it easy for people to live at greater distances from the services of the town.
- Bishop's Cleeve is targeted by Tewkesbury district council as a location for residential development, in order to protect other nearby villages, e.g. Winchcombe.

Places
For a named settlement within an LEDC:
- describe its growth or decline
- explain the reasons for the growth or decline
- list problems and benefits associated with the growth or decline

Growth of rural settlements

Case study *continued*

- There are currently plans for up to 4000 new dwellings to the north west of Bishop's Cleeve. One hundred homes are under construction on land currently owned by Dean Farm. The proposed development is needed to satisfy a rise in demand for housing in the region.

The effects of change
- The growth in population has eroded the village's character, residents however have banded together with the Parish Council to protect the community's interests and preserve its historic identity.
- There is now the necessary threshold population to support a number of services:
  - two supermarkets, Lidl and Tesco have recently been opened.
  - a new primary school is currently being constructed.
  - a youth club and local drama group.
  - a secondary school with a successful sixth form.
  - new development of retail outlets proposed for the year 2000.
- Unfortunately, new superstores have led to the closure of smaller village stores such as Budgens, which closed in late 1999.
- The continuing growth in Bishop's Cleeve has strengthened the sense of community.
- However, local objections to further development are strong and the Parish council is against large scale residential development.
- Further development to the north of the existing settlement will increase congestion on the A435.

Hints and Tips!
To look up Bishop's Cleeve on a map, see grid reference 96 27 on the OS map on page 107.

Exam practice – foundation level paper

(a) Describe the location of Southam (grid reference 973256). [2]

(b) Southam has grown mainly to the west of the B4632. Suggest reasons for this. [2]

(c) What shops are you likely to find in Cheltenham but not in the smaller towns on the map? [4]

(d) (i) Describe the layout of Bishop's Cleeve (grid reference 960275).

   (ii) For one feature of the layout, suggest why local residents may regard this feature as an advantage or disadvantage. [4]

(e) For an urban area you have studied which is growing or declining:
   (i) name and locate the urban area;
   (ii) describe how it is changing and suggest reasons for the change
   (iii) suggest what problems and/or opportunities the change has brought to the local population. [8]

[Total 20 marks]

Summary

Population and settlement

Theme 4 check list

	Confident	Not bad	Needs more work
Population distribution, structure and change			
I know the factors affecting global population distribution	☐	☐	☐
I know the factors affecting the population distribution of an LEDC and an MEDC	☐	☐	☐
I know the factors that affect birth rates, death rates and migration in an LEDC and an MEDC	☐	☐	☐
I know that the global population is changing	☐	☐	☐
I know that changes in birth rates, death rates and migration affects the population pyramid of a country	☐	☐	☐
I know about rural/urban migration	☐	☐	☐
I know about international migration	☐	☐	☐
The location and function of settlements			
I understand the reasons for the location of settlements	☐	☐	☐
I know that settlements of different sizes provide different goods and services	☐	☐	☐
The growth and decline of settlements			
I know why some settlements grow and declinie	☐	☐	☐
I can describe the benefits and problems linked with settlement growth or decline	☐	☐	☐
I understand what is meant by quality of life			
I know that changes in settlements can affect people's quality of life	☐	☐	☐
I can describe issues and conflicts that might come from changes in settlements	☐	☐	☐

Test Yourself

Tick the boxes – if you still do not understand seek help from your teacher.

Hints and Tips!

Write down the names of your chosen case studies. Ask your teacher to check your choices.

Know your case studies

Which real places have you studied as an example of:
- population distribution in an MEDC (not the EU) name and location _____
- population distribution in an LEDC   name and location _____
- the factors affecting birth rates, death rates, migration in an MEDC (not the EU)   name and location _____
- the factors affecting birth rates, death rates, migration in an LEDC   name and location _____
- the change in the balance between rural and urban population in an LEDC   name and location _____
- growth or decline of a settlement in an LEDC   name and location _____
- growth or decline of a settlement in the EU   name and location _____
- issues and conflicts coming from changes in a settlement in the EU   name and location _____

Comparing regions

Regions are parts of countries that have distinctive characteristics. You may be required to describe regions or to compare and contrast different regions you have studied in an EU country, a named MEDC or an LEDC. There are many aspects of a region that you can discuss but you should be prepared to cover the following:
- climate
- physical features
- population
- settlement
- economic activity.

When comparing two regions it is important to emphasize the similarities and differences. Never write separate descriptions of each region; you are unlikely to gain high marks by doing so.

Hints and Tips!

When describing a region always include specific facts and figures rather than giving a general, vague description. Learn facts such as annual rainfall, population density, economic structure. Presenting your answer in a table will help you to structure your revision successfully.

Know your case study

Kanto and Hokkaido: Japanese regions
- Japan is divided into 47 regions known as prefectures. These regions are similar to the counties of the UK.

Location
- Kanto is located on the southern Pacific coast of the main island of Honshu. Tokyo is its biggest city.
- Hokkaido is the most northerly of Japan's islands. Sapporo is its biggest city.

Climate
- The Kanto region has warm, wet summers with summer temperatures reaching over 30°C. September is generally the wettest month with a monthly average of over 216mm. Winters are much cooler and drier with temperatures ranging from 0 to 7°C and January rainfall averaging 49mm.
- Hokkaido in comparison has long cold winters with snow lasting from November to April. Summers are cool but drier than in Kanto.

Physical features
- The Kanto region covers an area just over 2000 square km. The region is dominated by the great Kanto Plain, a large, low-lying stretch of land. The north of the region is mountainous while the coastal areas are highly urbanized.
- Hokkaido is dominated by the Taisetsu-zan mountain range with several peaks over 2000m. Only 16 per cent of the island is urban and settlement is limited to the narrow coastal plain. The area has several major rivers including the Ishikari-gawa and Teshio-gawa surrounded by alluvial plains. The region also has volcanic hot springs. Hokkaido is much larger than the Kanto region with an area of 78,413 square km.

Population
- The total population of Kanto is approaching 40 million. There are nearly 12 million in Tokyo alone. The average population density in Kanto is over 5000 people per square km.
- Hokkaido currently has just over 5.5 million with an average population density of 72 people per square km.

Economic activity
- The urban economy of Kanto is dominated by tertiary industries. Secondary industries include microelectronics and auto vehicle manufacturing. Agriculture outside Tokyo includes dairy and fruit farming.
- Hokkaido specializes in agriculture including dairy farming, salmon and trout fisheries and trawling for scallops and crabs.

Comparing regions

	Region A:	Region B:
Climate		
Physical features		
Population		
Settlement		
Economic activity		
Evidence of reasons for growth/decline		

Test Yourself

Places

Copy and complete the table using information from two contrasting regions of an EU country, e.g. Lombardy and Basilicata in Italy or the Île de France and Provence.

Places

In section A of the final exam you will have to answer two of three questions provided. You will need to name and locate specific places, and be able to answer questions on some of the following: climate, physical features, population, settlement and economic activity.

The practice examination questions that follow are given at higher and foundation level.

Exam practice – higher level paper

This question is about LEDCs.

(a) Read the following paragraph.

> Bangladesh has a high population density. The country is mostly a flat low-lying delta, formed by deposition from the rivers Ganges and Brahmaputra, where severe disasters happen frequently. In May 1995 an estimated 9 metre high tide flooded 150 km inland across the delta, killing 40 000 people. Winds of 180 km/hr were recorded.

Identify three physical factors which combined to cause the disaster. [2]

(b) Explain how human factors may have increased the severity of the disaster. [2]

(c) Study the table below.

Country	GNP per capita in US dollars	Adult literacy %	Number of people per doctor	Energy used (kg. per capita oil equivalent)
Argentina	7 290	96	337	1 428
Bangladesh	220	36	6 615	65
Chad	200	45	60 415	5
Kenya	270	75	7 358	81
Libya	5 350	72	862	2 163
Mexico	3 750	89	663	1 311

Compare the quality of life for two of the LEDCs shown. [4]

(d) Explain the relationship shown in the table between GNP per capita and one of the other variables. [4]

(e) Governments in LEDCs often encourage foreign investment and aid.
Use named examples to suggest advantages and disadvantages for the people of LEDCs of such investment and aid. [8]

[Total 20 marks]

Exam practice – foundation level paper

This question is about LEDCs.

Read the following paragraph.

> Bangladesh has a high population density. The country is mostly a flat low-lying delta, formed by deposition from the rivers Ganges and Brahmaputra, where severe disasters happen frequently. In May 1995 an estimated 9 metre high tide flooded 150 km inland across the delta, killing 40 000 people. Winds of 180 km/hr were recorded.

(a) Name two physical factors mentioned which helped to cause the disaster. [2]

(b) Suggest two other possible reasons why the number of deaths was so high. [2]

(c) Study Fig. 1.

Country	GNP per capita*	Adult literacy %**	Number of people per doctor	Energy used***
Argentina	7 290	96	337	1 428
Australia	17 510	99	467	5 310
Bangladesh	220	36	6 615	65
Chad	200	45	60 415	5
Kenya	270	75	7 358	81
Libya	5 350	72	862	2 163
Mexico	3 750	89	663	1 311
UK	17 970	99	623	3 910
USA	24 750	99	408	7570

Key
* GNP per capita – the value, in US dollars, of what a country produces in a year, divided by the population.
** Adult literacy – the percentage of the adult population able to read and write.
*** Energy used – kilograms per capita oil equivalent.

▲ *Fig. 1 Quality of life*

(i) Name the three least economically developed countries.

(ii) What do the three countries have in common? [4]

(d) Study Fig. 2

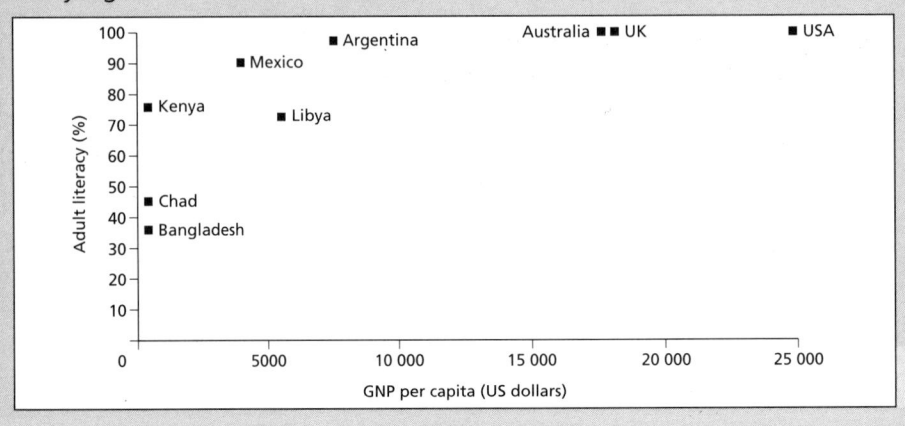

◀ *Fig. 2*

(i) Describe the relationship between GNP and adult literacy.
(ii) Suggest two reasons for the relationship you have described. [4]

(e) Study Fig.3

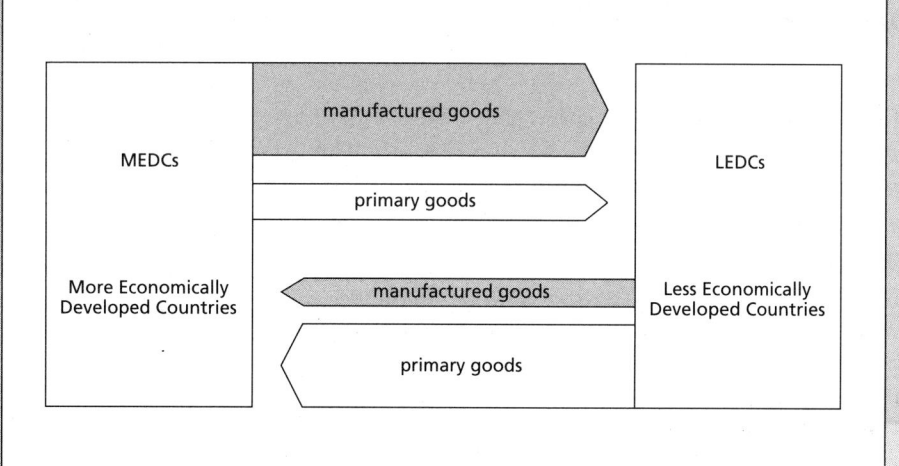

Fig. 3

(i) Use examples from LEDCs you have studied to help you explain the pattern of trade shown on the diagram.
(ii) For an LEDC country you have studied, describe how investment and aid has brought it either advantage or disadvantages. [8]

[Total 20 marks]

DME and practical skills

The Decision Making Exercise

What is the DME?
The DME is a new and exciting form of examination. The exam is taken in the second half of the spring term during the second year of study. The DME is worth 25 per cent of the total marks and is a very important part of your assessment.

What will the DME be about?
The DME is based on environmental issues associated with theme five – people's use of the world's resources. Past issues have included traffic management in the UK, rainforest management and the management of water resources. You will study related themes during the two-year course and will have background knowledge of the chosen issue. The issues chosen are contemporary and have an impact on society today. The DME gives you the opportunity to study the background to an environmental issue and explore the impact it has on real places (Section 1). You will also learn about and evaluate the alternative management options available (Section 2) and use your skills and knowledge to decide on the most appropriate way to resolve the issue and minimize conflict (Section 3).

How can you prepare for the exam?
The resource booklet on which the exercise is based will be made available to you three weeks before the exam. The three-week period should be used to study the resources and explore the chosen issue in depth. Your teacher will structure preparation sessions for you and it is important that you do not miss classes during this period.

The most important things to consider are:
1. **Can you use and understand all the resources?** If there are any resources you find difficult to interpret or unclear in any way you must seek advice from your teacher.
2. **Have you studied all the resources?** The exam questions may refer to specific resources but you should aim to refer to all the resources in your answers. If you have neglected certain resources you may be at a disadvantage in the exam.
3. **Do you understand the issue?** Make sure you have a clear understanding of the issue. Write yourself a summary using the following headings;
   - How does the issue affect local areas?
   - How are regions affected differently by the issue?
   - Are there any global links?
   - Who does the issue affect?
   - What are the viewpoints held by the different interest groups?
   - Are there any conflicts of interest generated by the issue?
   - What are the alternative ways of managing the issue?

Hints and Tips!
When exploring a possible management plan always consider social, economic and environmental effects in order to give a really balanced response.

Section 1: Background

Organizing your preparation

It may be useful to have a clear overview of all the resources. For each of the resources in turn describe the resource, e.g. 'A map showing temperature and rainfall patterns of the UK'. Then note down the key points drawn from the resource, e.g. 'The maps show that the south east has a warmer, drier climate than the north west'. Complete the table below.

▼ *Resource summaries*

Resource no.	Description	Key points

DME and practical skills

Section 2: Exploring the options

This section explores the options available to decision-makers. You must evaluate all the options presented. There are always alternative ways of managing the environment.

When studying the alternatives you must consider the:
- economic costs and benefits
- environmental costs and benefits
- social costs and benefits
- the sustainability of the option (what are the future implications?).

Try to produce a table like the one below.

Option no.	Economic costs and benefits	Environmental costs and benefits	Social costs and benefits	Sustainability and future implications

◀ *Breaking down the options*

Hints and Tips!

Evaluate means that you must consider the advantages **and** disadvantages of each option. Don't overemphasize the environmental impacts. A good evaluation will consider social, economic and environmental aspects. It is unlikely that any option will be completely advantageous. You must consider the balance of costs and benefits.

Hints and Tips!

It is also important to consider how the interest groups will respond to each of the options. Which option pleases the majority of people? Which option is likely to create the most objections?

Section 3: Making a decision

This section requires you to make a decision based on careful consideration of the information available in the resources and your own knowledge. The task in Section 3 of the exam can take many different forms.
1. You may be asked to choose the best option from a selection of choices based on certain criteria.
2. You may be asked to rank order a number of options.
3. You may be given a situation for which you must identify the most feasible solution.

When making a decision about the management of resources you must consider the following:
- Which option or combination of options offers the most benefits and least costs?
- Which option/options causes the least conflict?
- Which option/options offers the most sustainable solution?
- What problems may arise from the final decision and how can they be minimized?

Technique
1. Justify your decision by referring to the resources.
2. Don't waste time by copying out large chunks of text. A quick reference to the resource followed by your explanation will be adequate, e.g. 'Resource 9 indicates that……….'
3. Timing is very important. You will have half an hour on each section. If you spend too long on Sections 1 and 2 you may lose valuable marks on the final section.
4. On Section 3 your answer must reflect the task set. Make sure you read the instructions carefully. If you are told to refer to particular resources you must refer to them in your answer.
5. A good response will:
   - describe the best option
   - explain your reasons for choosing that option
   - describe any problems associated with that decision
   - suggest ways those problems can be overcome
   - explain why you have not chosen the alternatives.
6. You must state your decision first. If you leave the final decision until last you may run out of time and lose marks.

The diagram below outlines some of the important questions that a decision-maker must consider. Try answering them using your resource booklet.

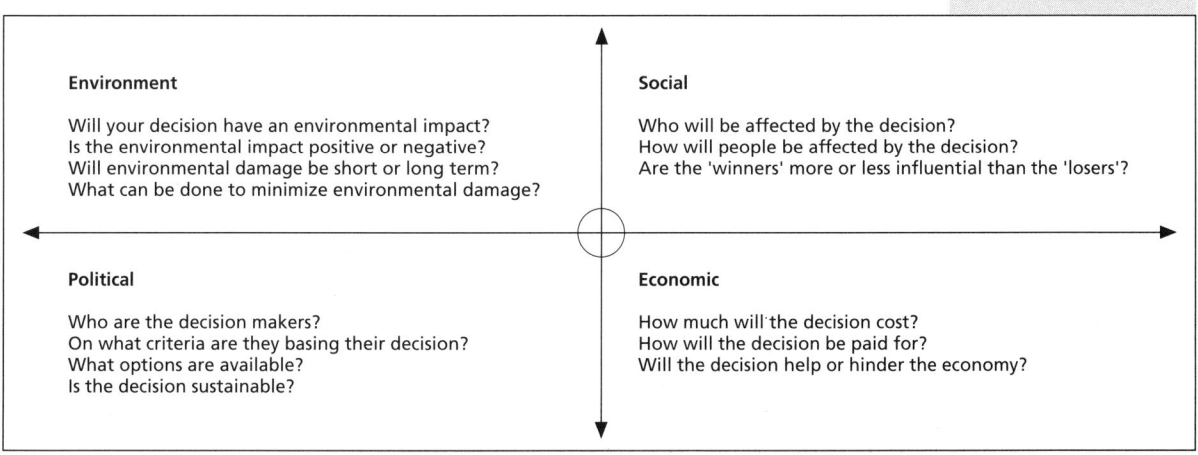

▼ *The decision-making compass*

Environment
Will your decision have an environmental impact?
Is the environmental impact positive or negative?
Will environmental damage be short or long term?
What can be done to minimize environmental damage?

Social
Who will be affected by the decision?
How will people be affected by the decision?
Are the 'winners' more or less influential than the 'losers'?

Political
Who are the decision makers?
On what criteria are they basing their decision?
What options are available?
Is the decision sustainable?

Economic
How much will the decision cost?
How will the decision be paid for?
Will the decision help or hinder the economy?

Practical skills

You will be expected to demonstrate skill in using and interpreting a variety of resources. Resources are used in the DME booklet and in the terminal examination. Resources that you may have to use include:
- a variety of graphs
- a variety of maps
- photographs
- satellite images
- cartoons.

Confidence in using these resources will save you time in the exam and help you to gain higher marks. This section will introduce you to a selection of these resources, give tips on how to use them and provide examples of how they may be used in the exam.

OS maps

You may be expected to use an OS map in the DME or your final exam. Candidates frequently shy away from the questions that refer to OS maps. This may be due to a lack of confidence in basic map skills. Using OS maps well depends on your ability to:
- use direction
- use scale
- use four figure, and six figure, grid references
- use a key
- interpret patterns (such as relief or settlement).

All this may seem rather daunting but these skills are all quite straightforward. Read the following paragraphs and then practise your map skills using the test yourself questions.

Direction

There are 360 degrees in a circle and 360 bearings on a compass. When using an OS map in the field you would use a compass and all 360 bearings. In the exam you will not be expected to have a compass but you will be expected to know the main compass points. The four main directions of North, South, East and West are easily learnt using the face of a clock. North is 12 o'clock, East is 3 o'clock, South is 6 o'clock, and West is 9 o'clock. Alternatively, you can use a simple rhyme such as **N**ever **E**at **S**hredded **W**heat, or **N**aughty **E**lephants **S**quirt **W**ater.

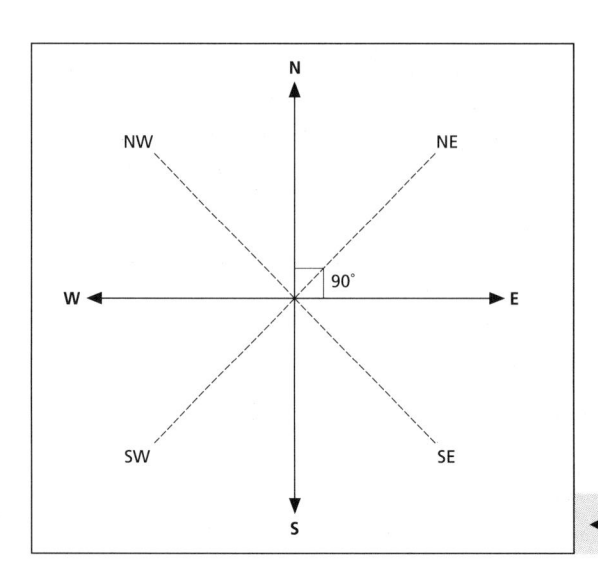

◀ Compass directions

Grid references

Grid references are used on OS maps to identify areas of one kilometre squared. All OS maps are divided into squares by two sets of lines. Eastings

Practical skills

are the vertical lines that run across the bottom of the map telling you how far east you have to go. Northings are the horizontal lines numbered up the sides of the map telling you how far north you have to go. You must always give the Eastings before the Northings.

Four figure grid references

Four figure grid references will pinpoint a square on the map. The most common mistake candidates make is using the wrong Eastings and Northings, even though they are looking in the correct square. An easy way to remember how to give the correct grid reference is to imagine a letter L which slots in to the bottom left-hand corner of the square. The stick of the L lies on the Easting and the Bottom of the L lies on the Northing.

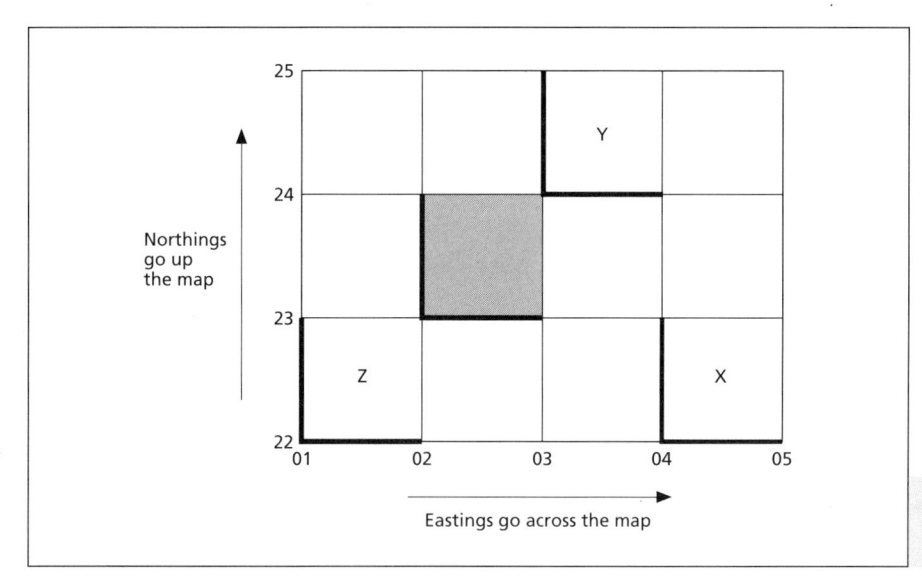

Test Yourself

Skills

The four figure grid reference for the shaded square is 02 23. The four figure grid reference for the letter X is 04 22. Can you give the grid reference for the Y and the Z?

◀ *Four figure grid references*

Six figure grid references

Six figure grid references are used to pinpoint a location within a square.
- You must imagine that each grid square is 10 by 10.
- Give the Easting and then count how many tenths east you must go.
- Give the Northing and then count how many tenths north you must go.

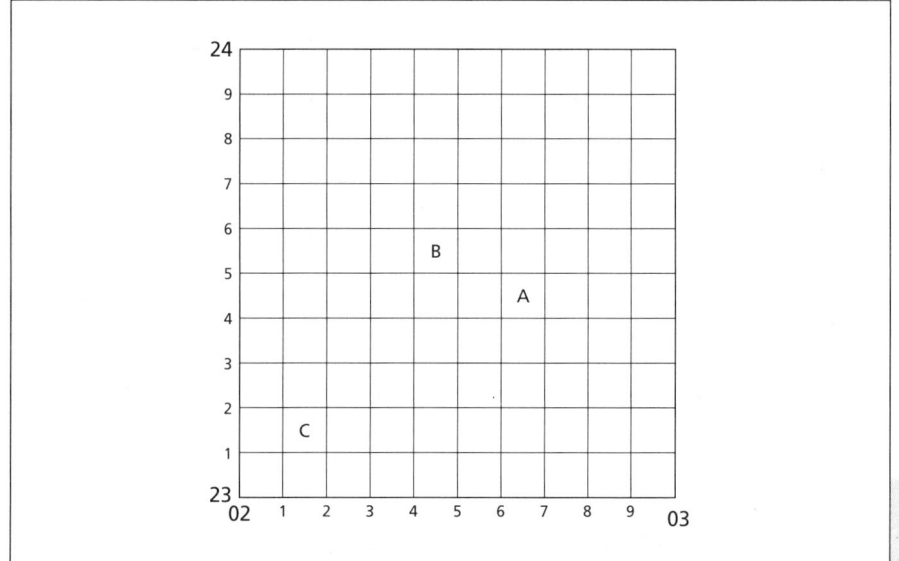

Test Yourself

Skill

The six figure grid reference for the letter A is 02**6** 23**4**. The six figure grid reference for the letter B is 02**4** 23**5**. Can you give the six figure grid reference for the letter C?

◀ *Six figure grid references*

DME and practical skills

Of course, on an OS map you have to imagine how many tenths east and north you have to go. The easiest way of doing this is to find the halfway mark (5/10) and work on or back from that point.

Distance and scale

You will find the scale of the map at the bottom of the key. On a 1:50,000 Landranger map 2cm is equal to 1km. Larger scale maps are also available. A 1:25,000 shows slightly more detail over a smaller area. On these maps 4cm is equal to 1km. It is a good idea to have a ruler in the exam to make calculating distances easier.

Relief and landforms

Height and relief is shown using contour lines. Contour lines are light brown or orange lines that join points of equal height. The lines are clearly numbered with heights given in metres above sea level. On a 1:50,000 Landranger map the contour interval is 10m. Contour lines can also be used to identify patterns in relief and slope type. Where contour lines are tightly packed together slopes are steep, where they are far apart the slope is gentle.

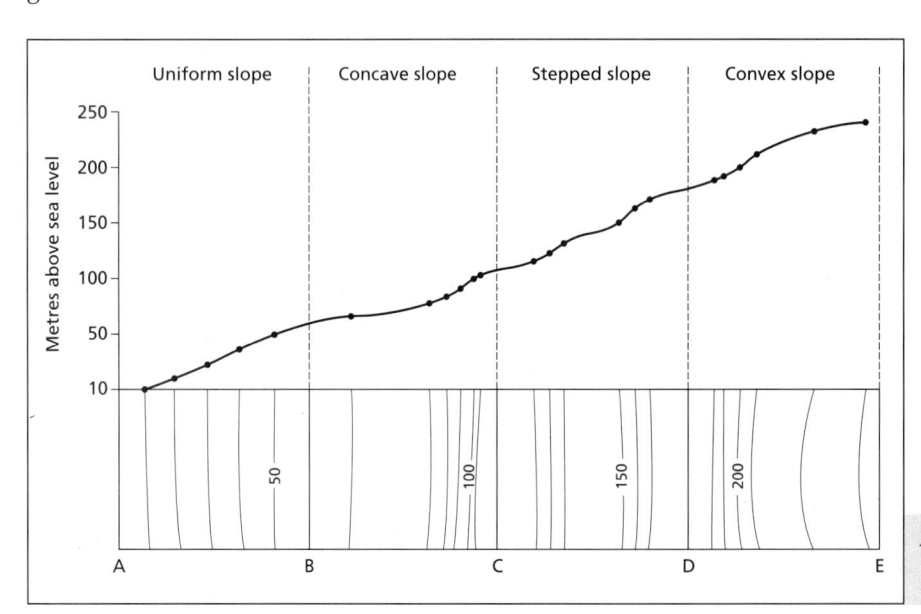

Hints and Tips!

On any OS map each grid square represents 1 km across and 1 km high.

◀ Contour lines and relief patterns

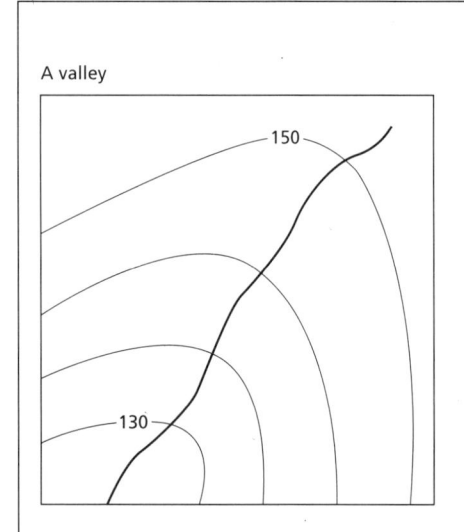

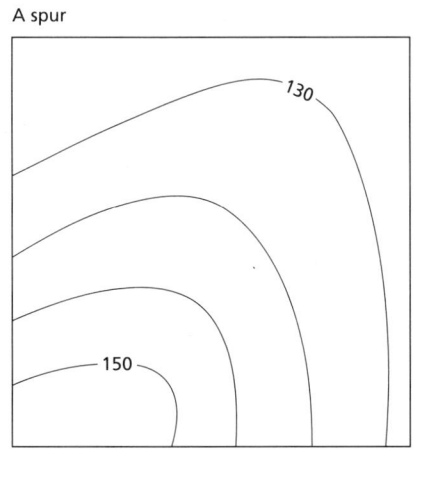

Hints and Tips!

Always double check whether the contours are increasing or decreasing. A valley and a spur look very similar but one is decreasing in height while the other is increasing in height.

◀ Land forms

Land use and key

All OS maps have a very user-friendly key. The key explains the symbols used on the map to indicate land use. You will always be given a key in the exam so you do not need to learn all the symbols but it is a good idea to practise using the key to describe land use in different grid squares.

Satellite images

Satellite images (see page 109) are used in a similar way to OS maps. They will usually be divided into grid squares to help you to pinpoint specific places. A key will be attached to help you identify different types of land use. Land use patterns can be easily identified on a satellite image. You must use your own awareness of geographical processes to explain these patterns.

> **Test Yourself — Themes**
>
> 1. Use the satellite image on page 109 to match up the correct land use types with the following grid squares:
>   - ploughed fields   9, D
>   - mountains   4, G
>   - city with docks   3, G
>   - volcano   12, C
>   - river meander   8, F
>   - industrial estates 7, D
>
> 2. Give two reasons why the lowland areas are ideal for cultivation.
>
> 3. Use the world satellite weather image on page 110 and label the ITCZ (Inter Tropical Convergence Zone), the sub-tropical high pressure zone and a low pressure system in the North Atlantic.

Photographs

Photographs (see page 111) may be used to illustrate a great number of geographical phenomena ranging from urban land use patterns to coastal processes and landforms. Effective use of photographs depends on your ability to recognize the patterns, and to understand the processes responsible for them. Photographs are frequently used in examinations to assess both your skills in identifying patterns and using knowledge of geographical processes to explain them. You should learn to interpret ground level photographs and those taken from the air.

Cartoons

Cartoons are an excellent way to depict complex geographical ideas. Again they are often provided to prompt your knowledge and understanding of patterns and processes. When using a cartoon you must consider:
- What is the broad idea on which the cartoon is based?
- Are any stereotypes depicted in the cartoon?
- Who or what do the characters represent?
- Is it a fair representation or is it biased in any way?

DME and practical skills

◀ A

◀ B

Aw, come on darlings – say cheese...

Graphs and charts

Throughout your GCSE course you will have used a wide variety of graphs and charts. You may well be expected to show your ability to read and interpret graphs in both the DME (explained on pages 103 to 106) and the final exam. Confidence in using graphs effectively can gain you valuable marks in the exam. Do not be put off if you come across a type of graph you have not seen before.

Bar charts

Bar charts are probably the most straightforward type of graph used. Quite simply the values of different variables are shown by the height of the bars. The horizontal axis gives the variables; the vertical axis shows the scale from which values can be calculated. To read a bar chart you must first select an appropriate variable then read

▶ Bar chart

Test Yourself

Themes

Study cartoon A opposite.

1. What is the cartoon showing about the links between LEDCs and MEDCs?

2. Do you think the cartoonist thinks LEDCs are treated fairly by the MEDCs? Give reasons for your answer.

3. What is cartoon B suggesting about the impact of tourism on LEDCs? How far do you support this point of view?

Hints and Tips!

When asked to refer to a graph or chart your answer should include evidence from the resource. A good candidate will describe patterns and back these up with evidence from the graph.

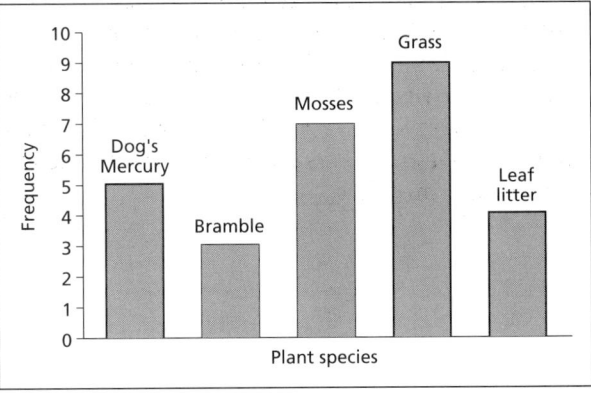

across to the vertical axis. It is important that you study the scale before answering a question. Some bar charts may not label the variables on the horizontal axis but may use a key instead. If this is the case you must study the key before using the graph to gain a full understanding of what the graph is showing. The tallest bar shows the maximum value. The shortest bar shows the minimum value.

A divided bar chart is used in a similar way to a pie chart. The entire bar represents 100 per cent of the data used. The bar is then divided into a number of segments. The size of each segment shows the proportional value of each variable. The largest segment represents the largest proportion of the data. Divided bar charts are frequently used to illustrate employment structures of different countries.

▲ *Divided bar chart*

Pie charts

A pie chart is a graph that is divided into segments. Each variable is shown as a proportion of a whole. The whole pie (the full 360 degrees) has a value of 100 per cent. 1 per cent is shown as 3.6 degrees. Although a protractor will help to read a pie chart accurately it is possible to estimate values. If a whole pie is 100 per cent, then a quarter of a pie is 25 per cent, half a pie is 50 per cent, three-quarters of a pie is 75 per cent.

Often pie charts are used on maps. This allows you to compare information from a number of different places. Although maps like this may appear rather complicated you only need to be able to read pie charts.

Study the pie chart opposite: the largest segment represents the most common residential type; the smallest segment represents the least common.

▲ *Pie chart*

Proportional circles

Proportional circles use area to show different values. The size of the circle is directly related to the value of the variable being used. The largest value is represented by the largest circle; the smallest value will be shown by the smallest circle. A key will generally accompany a proportional circle chart and you must study it closely in order to understand the scale being used.

Proportional circles are often added to maps to indicate patterns in regions or countries, such as population size, value of trade, or frequency of natural disasters. Whatever the information shown, the principle is the same. However, pupils often lose marks through failing to study the diagrams closely enough. Always double-check your answers to avoid making unnecessary mistakes.

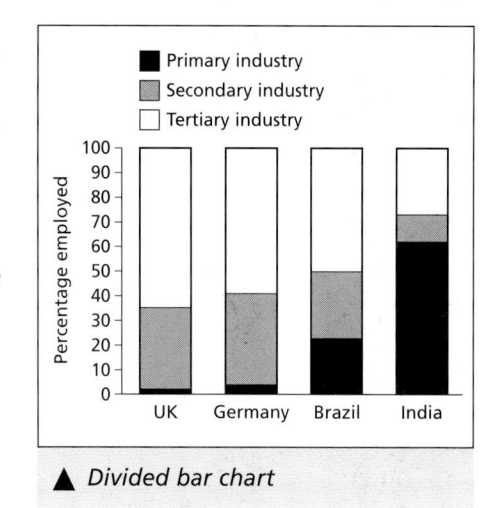

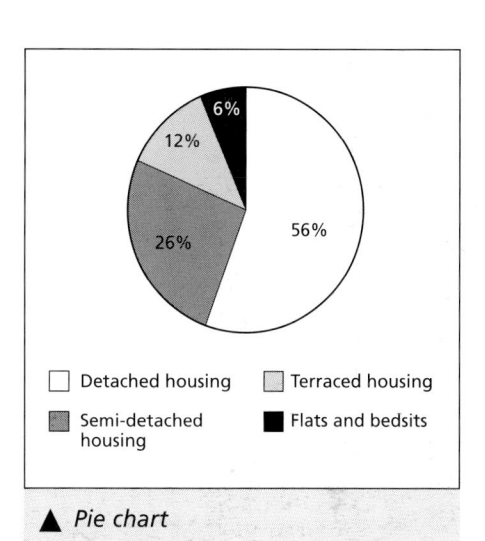

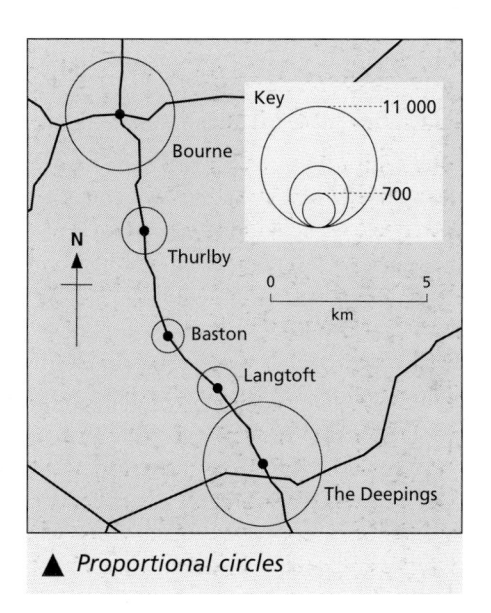

▲ *Proportional circles*

Line graphs

Line graphs are used to show how something changes over a period of time or over distance. Common uses of line graphs include temperature change and population change. Line graphs generally show the time interval on the horizontal axis and use the vertical axis to plot the variable. Scales may vary and it is important that you study the scale in order to read the graph accurately. You may be asked to identify:

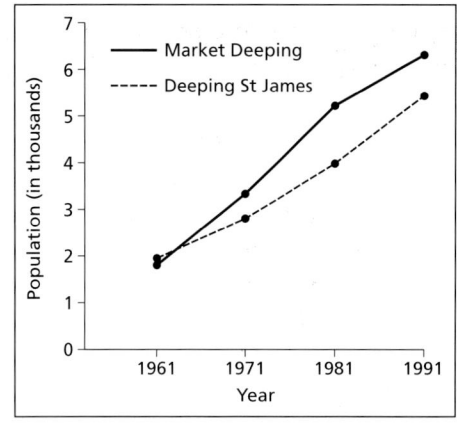

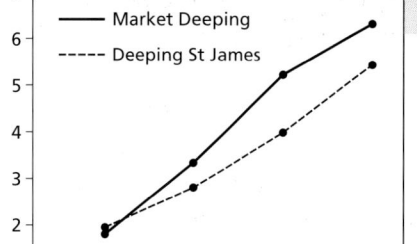

◀ Line graph

Hints and Tips!
A steep line indicates a rapid change, a more gently sloping line suggests a gradual change.

Hints and Tips!
When asked to interpret or describe the trends of a graph, never work through every stage of it. Summarize the whole graph.

- the minimum and maximum values by giving the highest and lowest points on the graph
- the rate of change by calculating the change in value over a given time interval
- the pattern of change by describing the nature of the increase and decrease over the whole period shown.

Scatter graphs

Scatter graphs are used to show the relationship or correlation between two sets of data. If one value increases as the other increases it suggests a positive correlation. If one set of data decreases as the other increases it suggests a negative correlation. If a random pattern is produced it suggests there is no correlation. However, a positive correlation does not necessarily indicate a direct cause and effect relationship between the two sets of data. When interpreting a scatter graph you must also think of other factors that could affect the pattern. It may show a clear pattern with one or two values that appear to stand out. These values are called residuals or anomalies. You may be asked to identify these values and explain why they are there.

▼ Scatter graph and (below) triangular graph

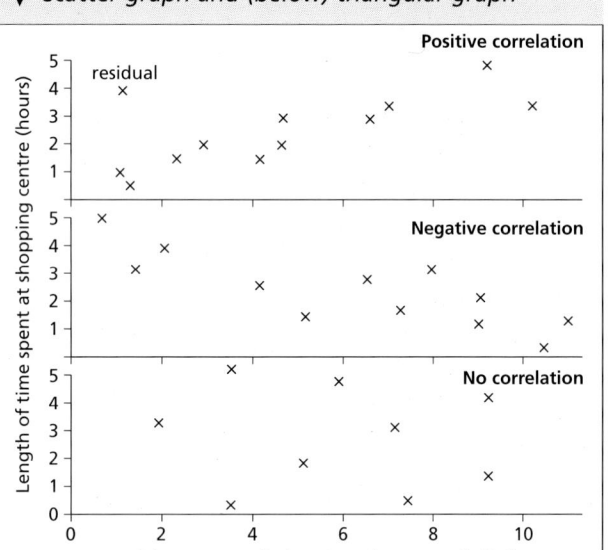

Triangular graphs

It may be necessary to plot three variables on the same graph. Where this is the case you may use a triangular graph. Each axis is of equal length and must have the same scale. Generally each side is divided into 100 per cent and the values are plotted as percentages. These graphs are often used to show the employment structure of a country but can be used to plot any set of three relative variables. Triangular graphs often put candidates off questions in exams as they appear to be very complex. In reality however, by reading one value at a time they are relatively straightforward. The most common mistake is beginning at the wrong end of the axis so always check the scale carefully.

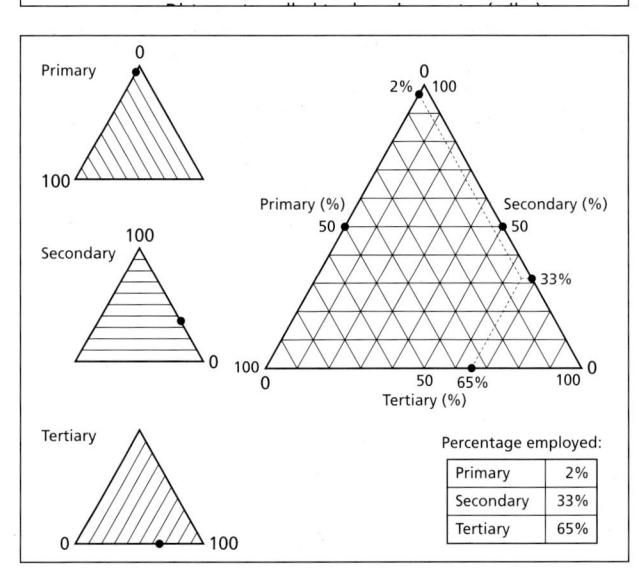

Percentage employed:

Primary	2%
Secondary	33%
Tertiary	65%

Reference section

▲ An Ordnance Survey map of the area around Cheltenham. Scale 1:50 000

© Crown copyright

Reference section

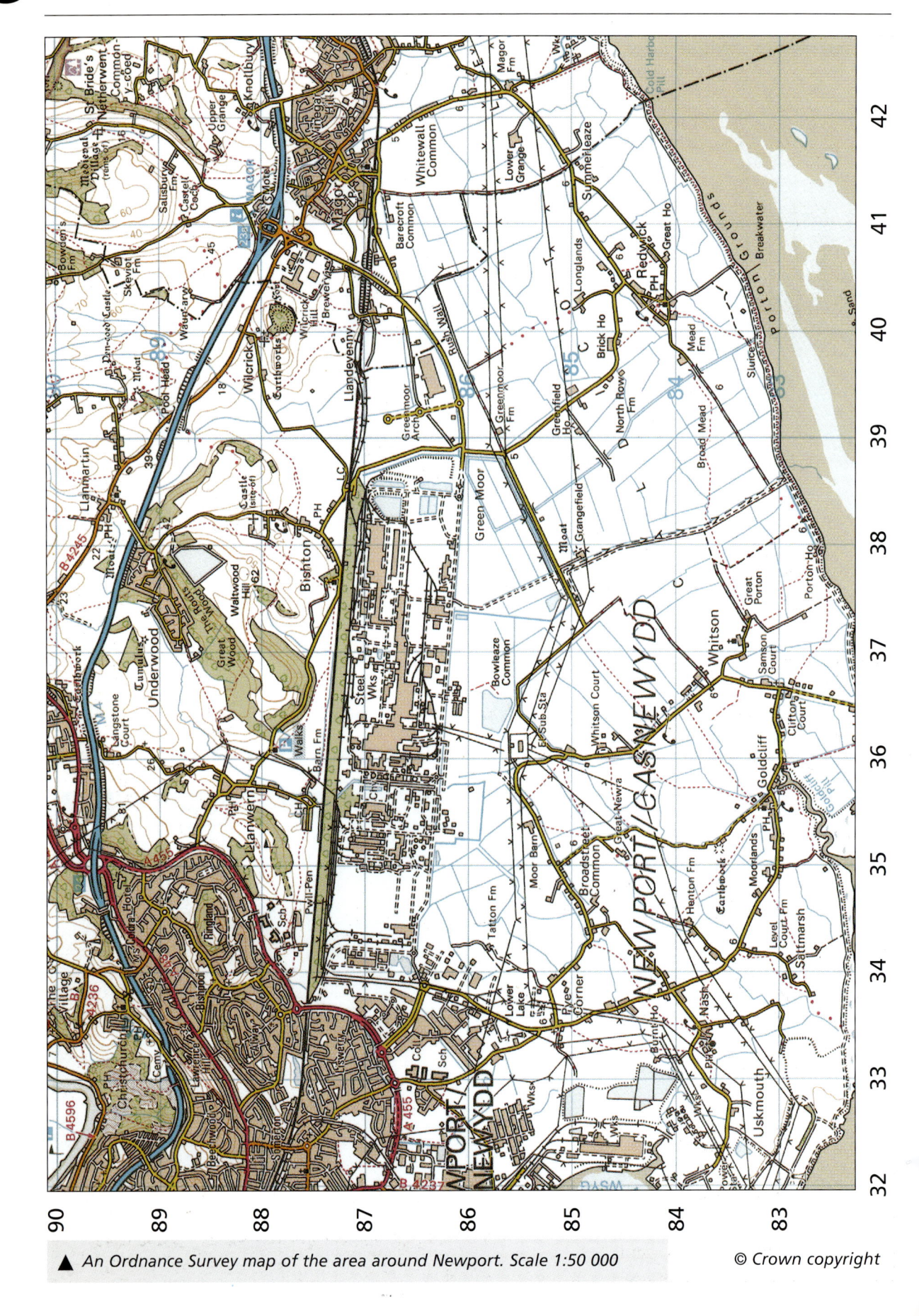

▲ An Ordnance Survey map of the area around Newport. Scale 1:50 000

© Crown copyright

Reference section

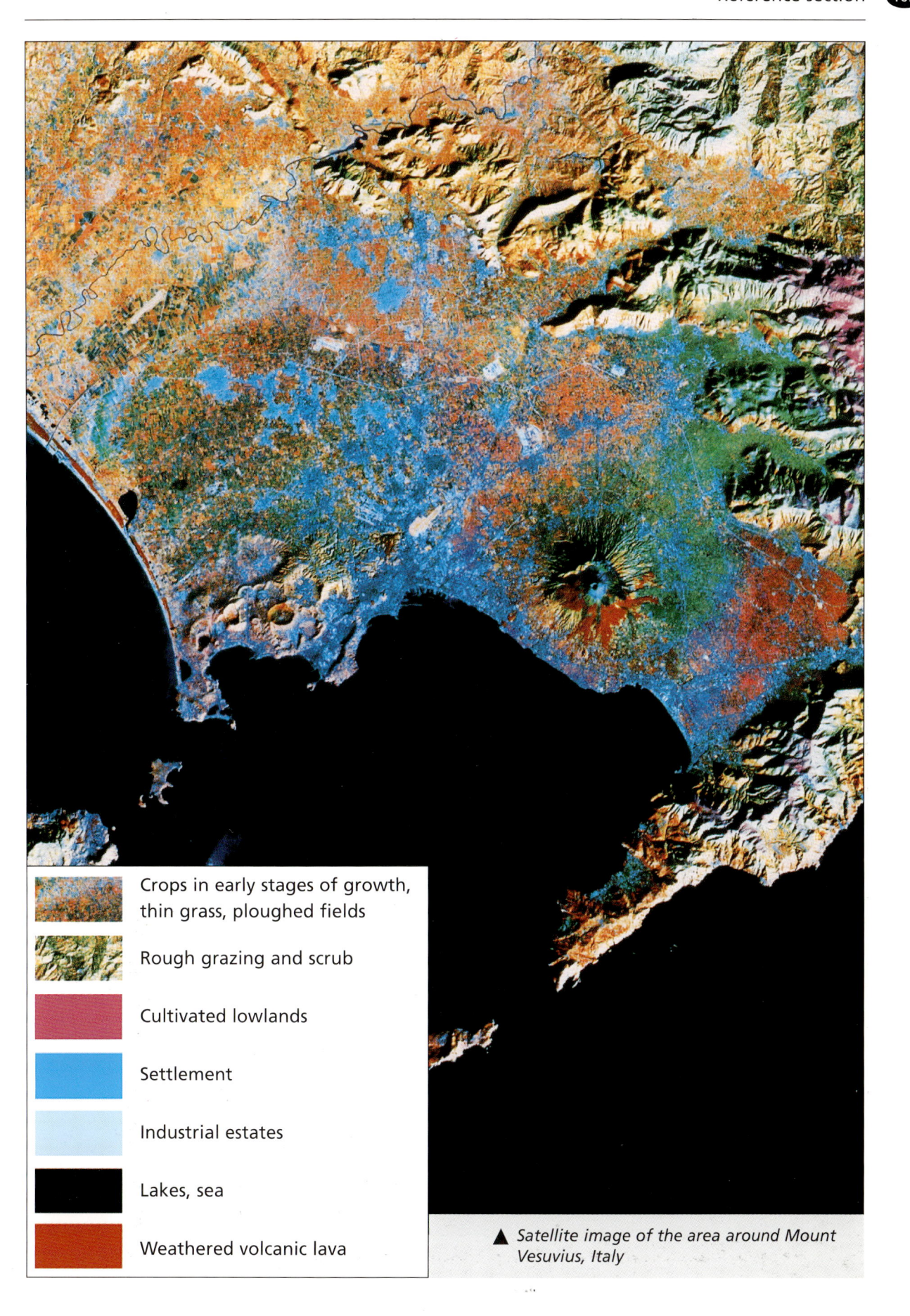

	Crops in early stages of growth, thin grass, ploughed fields
	Rough grazing and scrub
	Cultivated lowlands
	Settlement
	Industrial estates
	Lakes, sea
	Weathered volcanic lava

▲ *Satellite image of the area around Mount Vesuvius, Italy*

▲ Satellite image of the earth

Reference section

▲ *Favelas in Rio de Janeiro*

Test Yourself Themes

Study the photograph and answer the following questions.

1 Where would you expect to find areas of self-built housing like the one shown in the photograph?

2 Give two problems likely to be experienced by the residents.

3 Describe ways that governments have attempted to improve conditions in areas like the one shown.

Answers and advice on the exam

Exam technique: top tips

Terminal exam

1. Use the first 15 minutes to read through all the questions carefully. You must choose:
   - two questions from section A on either the EU, an MEDC or an LEDC.
   - one question from questions B4 and B5 on either Physical Systems and Environment or Natural Hazards and People.
   - one question from questions B6 and B7 on either Economic Systems and Development or Population and Settlement.
2. Before choosing your questions read every section. In each, e) is worth 8 out of 20 marks. There is nothing worse than getting to the final section of a question only to realize you do not know a suitable case study.
3. You should aim to spend 30 minutes on each question. Do not spend too long on one question as you will find it difficult to do well on the final question.
4. Take note of the number of marks available for each question and use it as a guide to how much time to spend/information to give.
5. Look for command words such as 'describe' and 'explain' (see pages 5-6). Make sure you respond to them correctly.
6. Do not take anything for granted. You must show the examiner exactly what you know. Write clearly and be specific. Don't assume the examiner will know what you mean.
7. If a question asks for a named example, make sure the first thing you write is the example you have chosen.
8. If you have named an example make sure you write about it and that you don't start giving information about a completely different place.
9. Give as much specific information, facts and figures as possible when using your case studies.

A word to Higher Paper candidates

1. Structure your answers carefully. Follow this step-by-step guide:
   a) Read the question carefully, noting any command words present.
   b) Break down the question into different sections.
   c) Ensure you deal adequately with each part of the question.

> **Example** For a region you have studied in an MEDC (outside the EU)
> a) name the MEDC and describe the location of your chosen region
> b) describe and explain how economic activity is changing.

Here you must:
1. name the MEDC
2. describe the location of the region within the country
3. describe changes in economic activity
4. explain (give reasons for) the changes you have identified.

A word to Foundation Paper candidates

1. You will write in an answer booklet where spaces have been provided for your answers. It is important that you write your answer in the correct spaces. If you run out of space do not use the space provided for the next section. Extra space is provided at the back of the booklet.
2. If you do use the additional space at the back of the booklet ensure you number the questions carefully so the examiner can easily identify the extra work.

Matching case studies to questions

Candidates lose marks every year because they choose inappropriate case studies.
- Make sure that if you are asked for a case study on a question about the EU, you choose an EU area.
- If you are asked for a case study in a question on LEDCs make sure you write about an LEDC.
- If you are asked for a case study in a question on MEDCs ensure that you write about an MEDC that is *not* in the EU.
- Make sure you know the difference between a neighbourhood, a settlement, a region, and a country.

Try to suggest the appropriate case study or studies for each of the following questions:

1. With reference to a named international migration:
   i) Explain why the migration took place.
   ii) Describe how the migration has affected the origin and destination.
2. For a named LEDC:
   i) Describe the regional variations in the level of development.
   ii) Explain why some regions are more developed than others.
3. For a named EU country, explain the regional variations in population distribution.
4. Name and locate a specific natural hazard you have studied.
5. With reference to examples you have studied, explain why natural hazards generally cause greater loss of life in LEDCs than they do in MEDCs.
6. Name two countries you have studied with contrasting birth rates and give reasons for the differences.
7. With reference to a named LEDC you have studied describe how governments can control the rate of population growth.
8. Compare and contrast two regions of an EU country you have studied.
9. For a named development project in an LEDC:
   i) Give information about the project.
   ii) Was the project a success? Give reasons for your answer.
10. For a named business or factory you have studied:
    i) Describe and explain its location.
    ii) Draw a labelled diagram of the economic system within the factory.
11. For a named example of a natural environment you have studied:
    i) Describe the links between the climate, vegetation and soil.
    ii) Describe how human activity may be damaging the natural systems.
12. For a settlement or part of a settlement you have studied which is either growing or declining:
    i) Describe the changes that are taking place.
    ii) Explain why the change has occurred.
13. For a named region you have studied, describe and explain recent changes in economic activity.

Model answers to exam practice questions

These answers are written using the examples included in the revision guide. You may wish to use case studies learnt at school. Read these answers to identify the type of information given. Then, using your own examples try to write your own answers.

Theme 1: Physical systems and environments
Foundation (page 26)

a) (i) 9923
   (ii) The Contours indicate 9923 is 310m above sea level. 9623 is 80m above sea level. The difference in altitude may lead to relief rainfall.
b) (i) 9623
   (ii) 9623 will have higher temperatures as it is at a lower altitude and will not be as exposed as 9923. Urban areas will also be warmer as buildings provide shelter and also release heat to the surrounding area. (Note – You are asked to give only one reason – choose from those offered above).
c) (i) Peak rainfall occurred on the 29th September.
       Peak streamflow occurred on the 1st of October.
   (ii) The peak stream flow occurs 2 days after peak rainfall due to the fact that it takes time for rainfall to reach the stream, via overland flow, throughflow and groundwater flow. Interception may also lead to this "lag-time" effect.
d) (i) The flow in the river was low prior to the rainfall because it is summer and evaporation will be high due to warm temperatures.
   (ii) The flow does not drop immediately back to its original level as water may be travelling via groundwater flow in the rock, this will reach the river gradually over a longer period.
e) (i) The Amazon Basin, Northern Brazil.
   (ii) The climate is tropical with temperatures ranging between 20-30° all year round. High temperatures result in convectional rainfall which produces a monthly average of 60mm. The heat and moisture result in high humidity levels.
       The vegetation is tropical rainforest. The forest has a distinct layer structure. The heat and moisture promotes year round growth which gives the forest an evergreen appearance. Leaves tend to have a thick waxy cuticle to protect the vegetation from excessive waterloss. The taller trees called emergents have butress roots above the ground to add support. Below ground the root system is shallow to absorb nutrients released from the litter layer.
   (iii) Human activity in the region includes HEP Dam Construction and large scale mining and farming.

Agriculture and mining in places like Carajas and Roraima has resulted in deforestation. This, along with commercial clear cutting for the timber industries removes the interception layer. Heavy rain falling on unprotected soil leaches away soil nutrients leaving it infertile and unable to support further vegetation growth. Rainforest is replaced with rough grassland, or secondary forest.

The reduction in evapotranspiration reduces local humidity levels and can result in drier conditions.

Dam building results in flooding of large areas of rainforest and the loss of valuable wildlife species.

Theme 1: Physical systems and environments
Higher (page 27)

(a) 9623 will have higher temperatures and less precipitation (snowfall) than 9923.
(b) Temperatures will be warmer as 9623 is low lying and the buildings will deflect the wind. Grid square 9923 will probably experience more snow in winter as the area is elevated (310m) and a lack of shelter means it is exposed to high winds. In winter any precipitation falling at high altitudes will fall as snow while in low-lying areas it will fall as rain or sleet.
This question required knowledge of microclimates.
(c) The weather in south-west Ireland is cloudy with moderate to strong winds and thunderstorms. This weather is due to the cold front which forces warm, moist air to rise quickly creating cumulo-nimbus clouds. When the hot and cold air collide in the

Model answers to exam practice questions

upper atmosphere thunder and lightning will occur. Air is sucked in to replace the rising air which creates strong winds.

Marks are awarded for a description of the weather conditions. Other than knowing how a cold front affects local weather to explain the conditions this requires no previous knowledge, only an ability to use the key accurately.

(d) The weather in southern England will change as the depression passes over. In the next few hours high cirrus clouds will begin to form as the warm front approaches. As the warm front passes over nimbus clouds will form producing steady rain. The temperature will rise as the warm air passes over. When the warm front has moved on the rain will ease and there may be breaks in the cloud. The next few hours will bring colder temperatures and heavy downpours and strong winds as the cold front passes over. These will gradually give way to showers and clearer weather until the next weather system moves in.

(e) (i) E.g., The Amazon rainforest in North West Brazil.

(ii) The climate is very constant. Temperatures are between 28-30°C all year round. Monthly rainfall is high averaging around 60mm. The constant temperatures encourage plant growth all year round. Vegetation is lush and green. Leaves have thick waxy cuticles to prevent excessive transpiration and drip tips to prevent water evaporating before it can be absorbed by the roots. The hot, moist climate results in rapid decomposition and leaching of nutrients out of the soil in heavy rain. Vegetation has a dense network of lateral roots close to the surface to absorb nutrients quickly. The vegetation also influences the climate. Evapotranspiration from the vegetation creates high humidity levels which lead to the wet conditions. Globally the vegetation of the rainforest helps to reduce global warming as carbon dioxide is absorbed during photosynthesis.

(iii) The Amazon rainforest may be under threat as a result of human activity. Dam building such as the Xingu HEP dam, mining at Carajas and resettlement programmes in Roraima are all threatening to upset the natural balance of the ecosystem. Deforestation leads to soil erosion and the siltation of rivers. Removal of vegetation takes with it up to 70 per cent of the nutrients in the environment. What is left is quickly leached out of the soil. Deforestation also disrupts the local hydrological cycle. Decreasing rates of transpiration result in arid conditions and the lush forest is replaced by dry grassland.

Theme 2: Natural hazards and people (page 44)

(a) (i) One
(ii) 10,000

To read a graph correctly, first note the labels on both axes – what is the graph showing? Then study any additional information such as labels or a key. The questions are not set to trick you but you must study the graph carefully. It is a good idea to double-check your answer before moving on to the next question.

(b) Most types of transport accidents occur more frequently than natural disasters (with the exception of railway accidents which have a similar frequency). However, the number of deaths caused by natural disasters is greater than that caused by transport accidents.

Note that the question asks for a comparison of two things, frequency and casualties. To score the two marks you must ensure you comment on both.

(c) Both floods were serious events and caused widespread disruption and devastation. In social terms the 1927 flood was the worst, even though the 1993 flood covered a greater area, as several hundred people lost their lives compared with 47 in the 1993 disaster. People were probably less prepared for the 1927 flood as rainfall before the event had been normal. In 1993 the Mississippi basin had received four times the normal rainfall and floods should have been expected. However, though the 1993 flood might have been less of a social disaster, it caused far greater economic problems. The damage cost 11,000 million dollars compared with the 1927 flood which cost only 4400 million.

You are clearly told to study the resources provided and your answer should refer to the information.

(d) Flood control schemes bring many benefits and problems to people living on floodplains.

Benefits

- Dam building such as the Aswan dam on the Nile and the planned Three Gorges dam on the Yangtze in China prevent the regular

floods which cause devastation to settlements and agricultural land.
- The dams regulate the flow of water in the rivers and allow year-round irrigation and increase agricultural productivity.

Problems
- Flood protection schemes are often expensive and are often paid for out of public funds at the expense of other services.
- Dams, such as the Aswan, prevent the deposition of alluvium rich in minerals on farmland which may increase the need for expensive chemical fertilizers – a particular problem in LEDCs.
- Flood defences encourage development of floodplains and create a false sense of security which can often prove devastating if defences fail, as at St Louis in the 1993 Mississippi flood.
- The straightening of river channels to alleviate flooding often increases the risk of flooding downstream. This also increases the risk of bank erosion which may threaten riverside land use.

This question is worth four marks and you should plan on spending about six minutes on it. To score full marks you must give examples of benefits and problems. A good answer will explain or expand on each point made or refer to a specific example.

(e) (i) E.g., The eruption of Mount Pinatubo on the 12 June 1991.
Mount Pinatubo is located on the Island of Luzon, the most northerly of the Philippine islands. The volcano is approximately 80km to the north-west of Manila, the capital city.

(ii) The volcano is located on a destructive plate boundary where the oceanic Philippine Plate is subducting beneath the lighter continental Eurasian Plate. The sinking plate melts creating pressure in the mantle. As this pressure builds up magma is forced to rise through weaknesses in the crust. Hot gases built up in the main vent causing a massive eruption.

(iii) The US Geological Survey set up an observation station following signs of volcanic activity in the Spring of 1991. Seismometers were set up to monitor earthquake activity and tiltmeters were established on the sides of the mountain to record changes in the ground surface. A hazard map was drawn indicating areas at greatest risk. On 3 June, following an increase in earthquake activity and gas emissions, scientists issued the first warning and evacuated 20,000 people. A further alert was issued on 7 June and a further 120,000 people were evacuated within a twelve-mile radius. It is difficult to control a volcanic eruption but many things were done to help those affected such as the provision of temporary shelters, fresh water, and emergency first aid.

Theme 3: Economic systems and development (page 69)

(a) (i) Nigeria
(ii) South Korea

(b) Three headings which could be used to divide the countries are:
More developed = increase over 10,000
Newly industrialized = increase between 1000 and 10,000
Less developed = increase below 1000.

(c) Two reasons some countries have increased their GNP more rapidly than others are:
- The EU countries such as the UK and Italy have been able to increase their GNP by joining a trade block. Trade blocks remove tariffs on trade making goods cheaper. This makes trade easier and increases the value of exports.
- Some countries such as South Korea and other NICs have increased their GNP through inward investment and import substitution (producing imports themselves). Using aid from the USA, South Korea invested in its manufacturing base such as steel and high-tech industries, increasing the value of exports.

You could also discuss the value of tourism in countries such as Tanzania. Oil and other valuable minerals have helped countries like Saudi Arabia and other OPEC nations to develop their economies.

(d) (i) Choose any two indicators from: literacy, life expectancy, infant mortality, birth rates, death rates, doctor/patient ratio, energy consumption, daily calorie intake, average income.

(ii) Choosing any of the indicators above will indicate the level of social development in a country, and help to show the quality of life in the country rather than purely economic development. However, using any of these indicators only gives us information about the average conditions and does not show us how the wealth and services are distributed within the population. These indicators also fail to show regional inequalities in the level of development.

(e) (i) E.g., South Wales in the UK.

(ii) The main changes in economic activity in South Wales are a decline in traditional industries such as coal mining and steel production and growth in footloose manufacturing companies, particularly micro-electronics. The steel industry declined as local supplies of limestone and iron ore were exhausted. Competition from countries such as South Korea that produced steel more cheaply due to cheap labour hit British steel production hard. A world recession meant that demand for steel fell. Most of the steelworks in the region closed, with the exception of Llanwern integrated steelworks. The growth of new footloose industries is mainly due to government policy. The government and the EU has offered financial incentives such as set-up grants, cheap rents and free training to attract new firms to the area. Other factors such as good road and rail links, flat land, and a cheap workforce have attracted companies such as Sony to Bridgend and Bosch to Miskin. Agglomeration (the build up of other factories) is also important as components produced in one factory supply another.

(iii) These changes have affected the quality of life in many ways. The environment is much cleaner – many of the derelict industrial sites have been landscaped and the new industries are cleaner. However, the new companies cannot offer employment on the same scale as the coal and steel industries and high unemployment is still a problem. The new companies favour sites along the M4, while the valleys are still very depressed. Many young people have left the valleys in search of work. This depopulation has a knock-on effect in the community as services and shops close down in valley towns such as Ebbw Vale.

Theme 4: Population and settlement Foundation (page 89)

(a) Southam is located to the NE of Cheltenham on the B4632. The village is approximately 1 km south of Bishops Cleeve and lies at the foot of Cleeve Hill.
Note: A good answer here describes the location of Southam in relation to other features. A good candidate will make clear use of the map evidence.

(b) The village of Southam has grown to the west of the B4632, as the land to the west is flatter than the land to the east, which rises sharply up the hill.

(c) Shops found in Cheltenham, but not the smaller towns on the map, will be high order shops selling either costly items such as furniture, or those purchased infrequently such as jewelry. Shops with a high population threshold such as department stores like Marks & Spencer and Bhs will also locate in the larger settlement but not in smaller towns and villages.
Note: A good answer requires a sound knowledge of settlement hierarchy and the sphere of influence of different functions.

(d) (i) Candidates should note the predominance of Cul-de-sacs in the settlement of Bishops Cleeve. These are linked with a few through roads.

(ii) Local residents may view this as an advantage as Cul-de-sacs are quieter and safer with no through traffic. The layout may also produce some disadvantages however as the through roads may get quite congested and busy.

(e) (i) Bishops Cleeve is approximately 3 km to the north of Cheltenham in the UK.
Note: You could also use an example from an LEDC such as São Paulo in the south east of Brazil – see page 90 for extra information.

(ii) Bishops Cleeve is growing steadily and is now populated by 4000 people. The village is earmarked for several new housing developments which may double the population.
The growth of Bishops Cleeve is mainly due to counter urbanization as people move out of the nearby city of Cheltenham into more rural residential locations. This trend has been facilitated by the increase in car ownership, which allows people to live further from the city. Bishops Cleeve is popular as it is connected to the city by the

A435 and is only a short distance for commuters to travel.

(iii) This growth has led to problems and opportunities.
- Problems such as increased traffic in and around Bishops Cleeve, particularly on the A435, causing congestion and noise for local residents.
- Demand for housing has driven up house prices forcing many low-income households to seek accommodation in the city.
- However benefits have also emerged. The rise in population has provided the necessary threshold for new functions to open. These include two new supermarkets that provide goods at a lower cost and at greater convenience.
- The rise population may result in the opening of a new railway station.
- The growing population has breathed life into the community supporting local schools, youth clubs, drama groups and local businesses. When many small rural primary schools are closing, Bishops Cleeve is due to open a second.

Places – higher (page 93)

(a) The flat, low lying delta, the 9 metre high tide and strong winds are all physical factors that contributed to this disaster.
Note: Physical factors are those that occur naturally and are not brought about as a result of human intervention.

(b) Human factors that may have increased the severity of the disaster include:
- high population density on the delta which resulted in greater loss of life;
- a lack of investment in flood prevention measures left much of the delta relatively unprotected;
- poorly equipped emergency services that result in slow and ineffective rescue efforts.

Note: For 2 marks you need to give two simple suggestions or select one but develop your point with a detailed explanation.

(c) *Note: You can choose any 2 of the LEDCs listed but it makes sense to select 2 with noticeable differences in quality of life.*

The data shows that quality of life is higher in Argentina than it is in Bangladesh. Firstly, GNP per capita is over $7000 more in Argentina than it is in Bangladesh. This means that people in Argentina are more able to afford a higher standard of living. It also suggests that there is a chance of manufacturing employment in Argentina whilst the low GNP per capita in Bangladesh suggests the economy is dominated by low paid primary employment such as subsistence farming.

Adult literacy rates are nearly three times higher in Argentina than in Bangladesh. This not only suggests a better education system but also suggests people in Argentina are more skilled and have better opportunities for securing well-paid employment. The relatively low literacy rate in Bangladesh suggests many people will be restricted to low-paid unskilled work.

The number of people per doctor in Bangladesh is 6615 compared with only 337 in Argentina. This suggests the investment in health services is higher in Argentina and as a result quality of treatment patients receive will be better.

The unfavorable doctor: Patient rates in Bangladesh will result in poor treatment and possibly higher levels of preventable deaths.

Note: You should show clear use of at least 3 sets of data provided and explain the consequences the statistics have on quality of life.

(d) The relationship between GNP per capita and energy consumption per capita displays a strong positive correlation. Put simply as GNP increases, so does the amount of energy consumed. (Only Libya differs as although GNP is ranked 2nd, it has the highest energy consumption.) This pattern is due to several factors:
- higher incomes suggest manufacturing industry features in the economy
- manufacturing processes tend to consume more energy than primary production.

(e) Investment by MEDCs in LEDCs often involves multi-national companies.

One example of an MNC is Freeport McMoRan, an American mining company with operations spread all over the world. This company has invested heavily in mining operations in Irian Jaya (formerly Papua New Guinea), on Indonesian territory. Their mine at Grasberg is the biggest gold mine in the world and the second biggest copper mine. The company's investment brings many advantages and disadvantages to Indonesia. Firstly, the company pays tax to the Indonesian Government, which can be used for investment in developing other aspects of the economy. The company also supports local businesses by purchasing locally produced food and services where possible. The mine provides employment for thousands of local people and offers many financial benefits such as higher than average wages, free health care and education for workers.

Disadvantages of investment in Irian Jaya includes environmental damage such as destruction of rainforest and the pollution of river systems with tailings. The new employment structure can increase differences between rich and poor in the local communities – Aid also often results in disadvantages as well as advantages for LEDCs. Aid can often be "tied" in that it ties the LEDC into patterns of trade, which may not necessarily help their economy. The British Government paid for the construction of the Pergau Dam in Kelantan, Malyasia. In return for the low interest loan the Malaysian Government agreed to buy arms from Britain, money, which could have been better, spent on developing their economy or on social developments such as health and education. The dam, which was intended to produce hydroelectricity and reduce the country's dependence on fossil fuel imports, has proved unreliable due to fluctuating river levels.

Note: For full 8 marks you would be expected to give specific examples of places you have studied and develop at least 2 advantages and 2 disadvantages.

Places – foundation (page 94)

(b) Choose from flat, low lying delta, a high tide and winds up to 180 km/hr.

(c) The population density is high. The country can't afford adequate flood prevention schemes.
  (i) Bangladesh, Kenya, Chad.
  (ii) All three have a very low GNP per capita, a relatively low adult literacy rate and a high number of people per doctor. They also have very low energy consumption

Note: For 4 marks you must name all three LEDCs required and give two features they have in common.

(d) (i) Literacy rates increase as GNP increases.
  (ii) High GNP means the country can invest in education resulting in improved literacy rates.

High literacy makes the workforce more productive. This results in higher GNP per capita.

(e) (i) The pattern of trade shown is that MEDCs export both manufactured goods and primary goods but the value of manufactured exports is higher than that of primary goods. This is because MEDCs can afford to process raw materials into manufactured products. These are then exported to LEDCs, which cannot afford to produce manufactured goods. The UK exports machinery and technology to Ghana and imports Cocoa beans.

LEDCs exports are dominated by primary goods – mainly metallic ones and food products. Manufactured goods are exported to MEDCs but the value of this trade is small. LEDCs such as Bangladesh export rice and jute and import machinery, textiles and technology.

Overall the diagram illustrates that exports from MEDCs to LEDCs are of greater value than exports from LEDCs to MEDCs. This suggests that trade patterns shown here benefit MEDCs more than LEDCs.

(ii) Indonesia is an LEDC that has received investment and aid from MEDCs. Freeport McMoRan, an American multi-national company, has invested in mining in Irian Jaya in Indonesia. They have a large gold and copper mine which has brought many advantages, both economic and social. Economic advantages include:

- The taxes Freeport McMoRan pay to the Indonesian Government provide reliable income of hard currency to be invested in the country's development.
- The company employs thousands of Indonesians in the mine, higher than average wages improve the standard of living.
- The company has invested in the infrastructure, building roads and a new airport that may attract other multi-national companies in the future.
- Social benefits include the provision of schooling and health care for workers in Grasberg.

Note: To gain high marks you need to discuss a range of advantages or disadvantages – giving both when only one is asked for will not gain you marks. And remember you need to write about real places to gain full marks.

Index

afforestation 41
agriculture 47-52
aid 63, 64
Amazon rainforest ecosystem 24-5
appropriate technology 64
assessment 4-5

birth rates 66, 75-9
Brazil 74, 82, 83
    see also Amazon rainforest
      ecosystem

charts 104-5
cities 86-7
    see also deurbanization;
      urbanization
climate 17
    British Isles 18-9
    change 22-3
    Equatorial 34
    global patterns 19-20
    influence on agriculture 47
coastal landscapes 10-11
commuting 88

death rates 66, 75-7
Decision Making Exercise (DME) 4-5, 96-9
deforestation 22, 23, 24, 25
deindustrialization 54-5, 57
Demographic Transition Model 76
deposition 12-16
depressions 21
deurbanization 87, 88
development 46, 63, 76
    see also LEDCs; MEDCs
diversification 50, 59
DME (Decision Making Exercise) 96-9
drainage basins 14-5
drought 40-41

earthquakes 30, 31, 32-4, 36-7
ecosystems 24-5, 49
environmental problems 52, 63, 64
    see also drought; floods; global
      warming; pollution; soil erosion
erosion 9, 10-12, 16
EU (European Union) 49-50, 81
examination advice 5-6, 112-9

farming 47-52
favelas 82, 111
floods 15, 22-3, 38-9

GDP (Gross Domestic Product) 46, 66, 68
glacial landscapes 12-15
global warming 22-3
GNP (Gross National Product) 46, 66, 69
graphs 104-6
Green Revolution 52
greenhouse effect 22-3
Gross Domestic Product (GDP) 46, 66, 68

Gross National Product (GNP) 46, 66, 68, 69

high-tech industries 46, 70, 71
hurricanes 42-3
hydrographs 15
hydrological cycle 13-15

industrial decline 54-5, 57, 87
industrial location 53-4
industries
    primary 46, 47-52
    quaternary 46
    secondary 46, 53-56
    tertiary 46, 87
inner city areas 87, 88

Japan 34, 37, 51, 73, 79, 91

LEDCs (less economically developed
    countries) 66-7, 68
    agriculture 51-2
    aid 64
    impact of natural hazards 33, 37, 38, 39, 41, 43
    population characteristics 74, 76, 77-8
    tourism 62
    trade 65, 68
    urbanization 80, 82-3
less economically developed countries
    see LEDCs
living standards 66-8
    see also pull factors; push factors
low-pressure systems 21
    see also hurricanes

map skills 100-3
MEDCs (more economically developed
    countries) 66-7
    see also EU; Japan; UK; USA
    aid 64
    carbon dioxide emissions 22
    deindustrialization 54-5, 57
    deurbanization 87-8
    impact of natural hazards 33, 34, 36, 37
    population characteristics 74, 76, 79
    trade 65
microclimate 17
migration 65, 80, 84
more economically developed countries
    see MEDCs
multinational companies (MNCs) 64
multiplier effect 53, 62

natural hazards 29-45

OS map skills 100-3

plate tectonics 30-3
pollution 22, 49, 52
population
    change 76-9
    control 78

density 72, 73
distribution 72-4
structure 75-6
population pyramids 75-6
primary industries 46, 47-52
    agriculture 47-52
pull factors, migration 80, 81, 90
push factors, migration 70, 80, 81, 82

quaternary industries 46

rainfall, types 20
regions 54, 91
revision advice 6-7
river basins 14-15
rivers
    landforms 16-18
    processes 16
rural depopulation 51, 61
rural development schemes 83
rural settlements 88
rural to urban migration 61, 82, 83

satellite images 103, 109, 110
scale 102
secondary industries 46, 53-6
services, settlements 86, 88
settlements 85-90
soil erosion 40, 41, 49
squatter settlements 82, 83, 111
standards of living 66-8
    see also pull factors; push factors
systems approach 20, 46, 47-8

tertiary industries 46, 94, 88

tourism 62
trade 65, 67
tropical rainforest ecosystem 24-5
tropical storms 42-43

UK (United Kingdom)
    agriculture 48-50
    climate 18-9
    deurbanization 87
    drought 40
    industrial changes, South Wales 54-6
    population change 79
unemployment 54, 55
United Kingdom see UK
United States of America see USA
urbanization 80, 82
USA (United States of America) 38, 39, 43

villages 88
volcanoes 30, 32, 35, 36

weather 17, 21
    see also hurricanes
weathering 9